KENOPANISHAD

KENOPANISHAD

M. HIRIYANNA

GYAN

Published by

Gyan Publishing House
5, Ansari Road
Daryaganj, New Delhi-110002
Phone: 011-47034999, 9811692060
E-mail: books@gyanbooks.com

Distribution Network
gyanbooks.com
India, USA, Canada, UK, Australia

ISBN: 978-93-6920-442-7 (HB)

First Published, 1912

2nd Impression 2025

Printed at: Gyan Press, Delhi.

KENOPANISHAD
Author: M. HIRIYANNA

KÊNÔPANISHAD

WITH THE COMMENTARY

OF

SRÎ SANKARÂCHÂRYA

Translated into English

BY

M. HIRIYANNA, M.A.

SRIRANGAM:
SRI VANI VILAS PRESS,
1912.

NOTE.

THE two manuscripts referred to in the Note to the '*Îṣâvâsyôpanishad*' have been consulted in this translation also and the few variations in readings suggested are based on them. Many of the foot-notes are taken from the *Tîkâ* usually printed with the text of the *Bhâshya*. This *Tîkâ*, however, does not appear to be by *Ânandagiri* for more than one manuscript ascribes it to a different author.

MYSORE,
6th October 1912.

M. H.

INTRODUCTION.

The *Kènòpanishad* forms a part of the *Jaiminīya* or *Talavakâra Brâhmana* of the *Sâma Vêda*, and is, for that reason, also known as the *Talavakâròpanishad*. Its four *khandas* or sections divide themselves into two parts—the first part comprising sections i and ii which are in a metrical form, and the second, comprising sections iii and iv, which are in simple, stately prose. This difference in the outer form of the two parts corresponds with a difference in their subject-matter as well. The first part deals with the unqualified (*nirguṇa*) Brahman or the absolute principle underlying the world of appearances, while the second, treats of the qualified (*saguṇa*) Brahman or the *Îṣvara* of popular belief. Thus the present *Upanishad*, in its brief compass, takes into account both the phases of *Vèdântic* teaching and inculcates not merely the higher but also what is termed the 'lower knowledge' of Brahman. The first of these two kinds of knowledge is intended for persons who, seeing the unsubstantiality of the things of sense, withdraw their thoughts from the interests of everyday life and desire to realise the ultimate fact of the universe. The second kind of knowledge is meant for those who although deeply pious yet perceive but dimly the distinction between the transient and the eternal and are consequently unable to detach themselves from the ordinary work-a-day world. As may be expected there is also a well-marked distinction between the results which these two kinds of knowledge are calculated to produce. The higher knowledge of Brahman (*parâ vidyâ*) procures immediate liberation (*sadyômukti*), when the individual Self, 'fusing all its skirts' remerges in the Universal Being. The lower knowledge of Brahman (*aparâ vidyâ*), on the other hand, puts one in the right path that leads to deliverance eventually (*kramamukti*). For a long time, in this case, does the Self continue to exist individualised; but, at last, it acquires higher knowledge, and through that knowledge regains its identity with the Supreme.

The following is a summary of the teaching contained in the two parts—

(i) The first section opens with a question put to a teacher by a disciple who is convinced of the utter futility of relying on the passing things of experience and yearns after a permanent reality by devotion to which he may attain abiding peace. He accordingly desires to know whether such a permanent reality is implied in the manifold activities of the senses and the mind or whether these activities are, after all, wholly dependent upon the transient physical organism with which they are associated. The teacher denies the possibility of the physical organism—a mere 'thing of matter' —being an automaton and states that for the source of the functions of the various senses and the mind we must look elsewhere. This permanent source of their power is here termed Brahman which however, the teacher adds, cannot be expressed directly (*vâchyatayâ*) for it possesses no specific attributes by which it can be described (in words or figured in thought.) Brahman is, in other words, absolute and reason as well as sense-perception fail to compass it. It can however be referred to indirectly (*lakshyatayâ*) through adjuncts which, empirically speaking, constitute its limitations—*ṣrôtrasya ṣrôtram manasô manaḥ* and so on, which means that Brahman is the inmost essence—

the basal fact—of the various sensory perceptions and intellectual operations. The precise bearing of this indirect answer is hard to understand and the statement that Brahman lies beyond the reach of reason as well as sense-perception appears to throw doubt upon the very existence of the alleged reality. Therefore the teacher, relying on authentic tradition, proceeds to give a separate 'definition' of Brahman which by its negative import suggests that the permanent reality underlying the phenomenal universe and the individual Self are ultimately but one. This step in the course of teaching suddenly transforms into a positive reality what was hitherto an extraneous and unascertainable something hardly distinguishable from non-entity. Our consciousness of Brahman may continue to be *indefinite* but there can be no doubt that it has now become *positive* for, if Brahman be ultimately one with our own Self, we are under an intuitive obligation to recognise it, our Self being the one reality from which we cannot get away. This fundamental identity of Brahman with the empirical Self forms the central teaching of the *Vèdánta* and the fact that it is based on an ancient text indicates the immemorial character of that teaching. The closing verses of the section re-affirm, in resounding notes, this ancient truth—that god in the sense of a personality exterior to us does not exist.

Since Brahman is eventually the same as the individual Self, we may get an *immediate* apprehension of Brahman, but it can never be an *object* of knowledge. The absolute must ever remain unknowable and a Brahman *known* would be no Brahman at all. To remove possible misconceptions in this respect, the teacher, in the next section, elicits the real significance of the previous section from the disciple who has by a proper course of previous self-discipline fitted himself for receiving the highest truth, and has therefore grasped the full import of the teaching and has by due reflection and contemplation realised Brahman in himself. Though the second section is thus merely racapitulatory in character, it is important as containing a statement (stanza 4) which shows how Brahman is continually present to our mind and can therefore be recognised at every stage of the unending stream of our ordinary consciousness. Consciousness involves self-consciousness, and, the Self being in reality identical with Brahman, every mode or sample of consciousness when divested of its 'phenomenal ingredient' gives us a glimpse of the ever persistent Reality which is 'without beginning or end, eternal, pure in form, devoid of distinction and the same in all.' It is, in fact, the *sole* unit of being. This monistic solution signifying that the material world and all the relations of life are mere figments *(kalpana)* indicates that the way to abiding peace lies in getting beyond them and realising the Self or Brahman. *Bhûteshu bhûteshu vichitya dhîrâḥ prêtya asmâllòkât amritâ bhavanti.*

(ii) In part ii the ground shifts from abstract philosophy to religion. Having indicated how Brahman can be cognised, the *Upanishad* now points out how it may be symbolised. By means of a well-chosen episode in which the highest deities figure, we are shown how the great *Îṣvara,* who has created the Universe, keeps a jealous watch over it and how the power that expresses itself through even the highest gods is but the reflex of the power of that *Îṣvara.* This episode is followed by the statement of a method of meditating upon *Îṣvara* or Brahman personified —as a preparation for that higher knowledge which alone can procure immediate release from the cycle of *ex*-istence. Meditation is but a means of mental discipline—a method of controlling the ever-shifting activity of the mind which has been so aptly described as 'a kaliedoscope of thoughts in constant motion.' By holding out certain proximate benefits as the reward of concentrating all one's thoughts on a single word or object—usually a symbol of the Most High—precepts relating to meditation help the gradual cultivation of that 'intensity of thought and serenity of temper,' which are necessary for suppressing the myriad shows of sense and perceiving the reality veiled by them.

It now remains only to refer to passage 8 of section iv which, though appearing in that section, does not really form a part of it. This passage, as shown in the commentary on iv, 7, occupies the position of an appendix to the whole *Upanishad* and mentions certain moral and intellectual qualities as the indispensable conditions of success in reaching the *Védântic* goal. These qualities are practically the same as what are termed the *sâdhanachatushṭayam* in systematic treatises on the *Vêdânta*. The great importance that is attached to this preliminary discipline is well-indicated by the legend of *Indra* and *Viròchana* to which reference is made more than once in the commentary, and it is necessary to lay special stress on such discipline for, without it, *Brahma-jignâsâ* degenerates into a mere theoretic curiosity which, according to the plan of the Vêdânta, cannot bring about the desired deliverance.

KENOPANISHAD

WITH THE COMMENTARY

OF

SRÎ SANKARÂCHÂRYA.

The ninth chapter (of the *Talavakâra Brâhmaṇa*) is begun in order to communicate the *Upanishad* treating of the supreme Brahman and opening with (the words) *kèna ishitam.* Prior to this, (the treatment of) all *karma* has been completed and likewise have been explained the meditations on *Prâṇa*[1]—the basis of all *karma*—as also those on *sâmans* subsidiary to *karma*. Immediately after, has also been indicated the contemplation of the *Gâyatrasâman*, followed by a genealogical list[2] (of the teachers of the *Sâma Vèda*)[3]. All this—*karma*

1. *Prâṇa* is the first-born principle of the Universe. Brahman, viewed as the source of creation, is termed *Iṣvara*. From *Iṣvara* is born *Prâṇa* or *Sûtrâtman* which is the universe itself but with its various elements only in their subtle or undeveloped form. *Prâṇa*, in its turn, gives rise to *Virât* or the Universe as we perceive it.

2. *Sishyâchâryasantânâvichchhèdo vamṣaḥ—Tîkâ.*

3. I put a full stop after *vamṣântam uktam* and omit *kâryam.*

and *upâsanâ*[1], heretofore explained,—when duly practised by one seeking liberation, with no selfish desire for rewards, tends to purity of mind. For one, however, that is desirous of rewards and is (thus) ignorant (of the real nature) of the Self,[2] *karma* —as laid down in the *Srutis* and *Smṛtis*—dissociated (from meditation)—obtains the 'southern path' leading to renewed birth. From yielding to natural *unṣâstraic* impulses, there results a falling down—from brute creation to plant life. Compare *Ch: Up*: (v. x. 8),—"Whoever do not follow either of these paths, continually return (to life) as petty beings and (of them it may be said), 'Be born and die.' This is the third place." There is also (in this matter) the following (authority of the) *Samhitâ* (as distinguished from the *Brâhmaṇa* in which occurs the passage just quoted)—'Three kinds of beings go by a farther course'[3]. In a person of purified mind, on the other hand,—with no selfish

---

1. It should be noted that *jnâna* here means *upâsanâ* and not the knowledge of Brahman, which, as will hereafter be shown, cannot be combined with *karma*.

2. I read *âtmajnânarahitasya* in place of *jnâna-rahitasya*.

3. The first eight *adhyâyas* of the *Talavakâra Brâhmaṇa*, as has been indicated in the commentary, deal with *karma* and *upâsanâ*. He who practises these two together, with a view to obtain their fruit, qualifies himself for what is known as the 'northern path' from which there is no return to this world. Individualised existence, how-

desires whatever,—who grows indifferent to the extraneous and transient correlation of end and means, there springs, through a distinctive culture arising from his deeds in this or former life, a desire to know the inner Self.[1] This point is indicated by the present *ṣruti* which is in the form of a dialogue beginning with *kèna ishitam.* The same has also been stated in *Kaṭha Up*: (iv, 1). —'The self-existent ruined the senses by turning them outwards; therefore (it is that man) looks outwards and not into himself. (Rarely, however,) some wise man turning his eyes inwards[2] and desir-

ever, continues in his case, long after death, but in a higher form, and eventually leads to *kramamukti* or slow advance towards complete liberation. If instead of thus practising both together, one performs *karma* alone without *upâsanâ*, the result will be a march on the 'southern path' which sooner or later leads to renewed existence on this earth. A third course is still open and that is to follow one's natural impulses without heeding what is prescribed or prohibited by the *Srutis* and *Smṛtis*. The result of such living will be a degradation—extending over practically infinite time—from man's rank to that of lower beings. Of these three courses, the first is not explicitly mentioned in the commentary but is implied.

1. *Vairâgya* is a necessary preliminary to a fruitful investigation of Brahman. The desire to know Brahman, when found alongside of worldly attachment, is a mere curiosity, and will not lead to salvation.—*Tîkâ.*

2. Here the expression, 'turning his eyes inwards' implies withdrawal from the world.

ing for immortality, sees the deeper Self.' So also in *Mund: Up:* (i. ii, 12)—'Having examined all the worlds attained by *karma*, a *Brâhmaṇa* should give up desires; for the eternal is not to be got through the ephemeral; and in order to know *that* (the eternal) he should, as a rule, approach, with fuel in hand, a teacher learned in the *Vèdas* and devoted to Brahman'. When thus grown indifferent (to wordly affairs) does one become able to know[1] the internal Self as also to study, cogitate and contemplate upon it; and not otherwise. And through such knowledge of the (identity of the) individual Self and Brahman, vanishes entirely nescience, the source of metempsychosis—the cause of desire and activity. Compare—'What delusion then, and what sorrow to one who discovers unity (*Îṣa Up*: 7); 'A knower of the Self overcomes grief' (*Ch: Up:* vii i 3); 'The heart's knots become untied; all doubts are solved; and all one's *karma* ends when one beholds that which is both cause and effect. (*Mund: Up*: ii. ii. 8).

If it be urged that the self-same result (*i. e.*, the removal of nescience) follows from knowledge combined with *karma*, (we reply,) 'No', for in the *Bṛhadâraṇyakòpanishad* such (combination) is said to produce a different result altogether. Thus (in the

1. *I. e.*, merely to apprehend the Self *intellectually* and not to *realise* it. Self-realisation follows *ṣravaṇa* &c., and does not precede them.

section) beginning with 'Let me have a wife'(i. iv. 17) the statement that 'Through' a son is attained this world, not by any *karma*; through *karma* the world of the manes; through knowledge, the world of the gods' (i. v. 16)—indicates the cause of the three-fold world *other than the Self*. The same Upanishad, again, while enjoining renunciation, assigns the following reason—'What have we to do with offspring—we to whom the Self is the only desired end?' (iv. iv. 22). The significance[1], of this reason is—'What have we to do with offspring, *karma* or knowledge combined with it, which (respectively) lead to the worlds of mortals, manes and gods and are not the means of attaining the world of the Self?' This three-fold world which is transient and attainable by(worldly)means is not what we seek; we desire that (end)which is inherent, unborn, undecaying, immortal, fearless— which neither increases nor decreases by *karma*. Being eternal, there is no possibility of its being attained by means other than the removal of nescience. Hence it means through a knowledge[2] of the (identity of the) individual and

1. The passage just quoted contains only the word *prajá* and the commentator explains it as implying also the other two means referred to, above—viz, *karma* and *vidyá* or 'lower knowledge' relating to deities.

2. See note 1, p. 2. *Vignána*, here also, means a mere intellectual apprehension of the Self. If it meant 'Self-realisation' there would be no need to prescribe renunciation of *karma*, for in that final stage, *sannyása* is a necessity

the Supreme Self, all desires have necessarily to be renounced. Further (such combination) is impossible since the knowledge that the individual Self is identical with the Supreme and *karma* are mutually exclusive. For co-existence of *karma* which recognises the distinctions of 'doer' and 'done' with knowledge relating to the identity of the individual Self with the Supreme, which negatives all such distinctions is certainly inconceivable. The knowledge of Brahman, depending as it does on an existing entity, cannot be contingent[1] upon what a person does or does not. Thus the *Upanishad* beginning with *kêna ishitam* (which follows the sections on *karma* and

---

(svataḥ prâptaḥ) and does not need to be prescribed. Renunciation is enjoined on one that has only a *mediate* perception or *parôkshajnâna* of the Self and endeavours after obtaining an *immediate* perception or *aparôkshajnâna* of it. *Brahmajnânasya anubhavâvasânatâsiddhayê parôksha-nischayapûrvakaḥ sannyâsaḥ kartavyaḥ.*—*Tîkâ.*

1. This is said in answer to a possible objection that from the view-point of knowledge, variety connot be altogether denied, as has been done in the previous statement, because the *Sruti* makes knowledge, just as it does *karma* also, the subject of an injunction (as *e. g.*, in *âtmâ vâ arê drashtavyaḥ)* and thereby implies variety, in the one case as in the other. The *advaitin* does not admit that knowledge can at all be enjoined for injunctions always have reference to that which can be accomplished through effort. *Jnâna*, for its manifestation, depends upon what is already accomplished and does not therefore need any effort. In sense-perception, for instance, the contact of the organ of

upāsanā) is for imparting the knowledge of the (identity of the) individual Self with the Supreme to one that has grown indifferent to the ends, attained by extraneous means,—whether those ends be visible (*i. e.*, attainable in this life) or invisible (*i. e.*, attainable in a future life). The statement in the form of a dialogue between a teacher and his disciple is, considering the subtle nature of the subject-matter, for making it easy of comprehension. It further suggests that this theme should not be investigated with the aid of (one's own) reason. Compare—'This knowledge is not to be attained through reason' (*Kaṭh: Up:* i. ii. 9). There are various other statements also (showing the necessity of a teacher) both in the *Srutis* and the *Smṛtis* such as—'He who has a teacher knows' (*Ch: Up:* vi. xiv. 2); 'Learnt only from a teacher will this knowledge yield the best (fruit)' (*Id.* iv. ix. 3); 'Know that by prostration etc. (*Bh. Gī.* iv. 34).

We should (here) imagine that some one finding no refuge, besides the inner Self, and seeking what is fearless, eternal, propitious and unchangeable, duly approached a teacher, devoted to Brahman, and questioned him as follows.—

sense with its object is sufficient to produce the impression and, given such contact, the impression is a necessary result. Similarly in the case of Brahma-knowledge, which also relates to an existing entity.

1. Sent forth by whose wish does the mind reach (its object)? By whom commanded does the chief *prána* move? At whose desire do (people) utter this speech? And what power is it that prompts the eye and the ear?

Kéna=by what agent? *ishitam*=*ishtam*=desired. *manaḥ*=(mind). *patati* *i. e.*, goes forth towards its object. Of the meanings of (the root) *ish*, 'frequency' and 'motion' being inapplicable here, the form—*ishitam*—in the text is to be understood as derived from (the same root with its third) meaning of 'desire'. The intermediate augment,—*it*—is an instance of vedic license.[1] *prèshitam* is also from the same (root) with the prefix *pra* added on, and means 'being commanded'. If only *prêshitam* were used here (and not *ishitam* also) there would arise questions about the nature of the sender and of sending, as—'By what sort of sender? What is the mode of sending?' If, on the other hand, *ishitam* also is used, both these (questions) disappear and it then specifically means—'Sent forth

1. The grammatically correct form is *ishta* and not *ishita* when the word is derived from '*ish*'—to desire. Hence this observation.

by whose mere wish?"[1] (Here, however, an opponent may say)—'If this were the meaning intended to be conveyed, the object would be gained by using *ishitam* alone and there would be no need for adding *prêshitam* as well. Further, it is but right to conclude that the use of an *extra* word signifies an *extra* idea and interpret the text as meaning—'Sent forth by whom—through desire or act or speech?' (We reply that), from the tenor of the questions (put by the disciple), this view cannot (be taken as right). This tenor makes it clear that the question is asked by one that feels a dislike for the aggregate of causes and effects—such as the body which is transient and caused,—and is desirous of knowing something which is different from it and is always constant and eternal. The question would otherwise be not significant at all because according to the current belief it is the aggregates such as the body, that impel by means of desire, speech and act. Even thus (the opponent may rejoin) the force of *prêshitam* has not been properly brought out. We reply—"Not so. This question is asked by one that is in doubt, which (circumstance) renders it clear that the word

---

1. By the word 'wish' should here be understood the mere *presence* of the Self, for it would be incorrect to attribute any 'wishing,' in the ordinary sense, to the Self. *Ichchâ mâtreṇa prayatnamantarêṇa sannidhimâtreṇa—Tîkâ.* The usual example given for illustrating influence from proximate presence is a magnet attracting a piece of iron.

prêshitam has a special significance here. It means—'Does direction proceed, as ordinarily believed, from the aggregate of causes and effects —like the body? or, Are mind and the like prompted by the mere presence of an independent principle distinct from that aggregate?' In order to indicate thus much both the modifying terms—*ishitam* and *prêshitam*—have to be used." Well, is it not (usually) admitted that the mind, being independent, reaches its objects of its own accord? In that case where is the relevance of the (disciple's) question? To this point we reply (as follows)—If mind were thus free to reach or avoid its objects, no one would think of harmful things. But (we know for a fact that) knowing a thing as bad, the mind desires it and, though checked, it sets about business which is imminent with misery. Hence it is appropriate to ask—'By whose wish &c.' *Kêna*=(by whom?). *prâṇaḥ*=(breath). *yuktaḥ*=commanded or induced. *praiti* *i. e.*, sets about its business. The epithet *prathamaḥ* is to be taken with *prâṇaḥ*, its activity being prior to that of all the senses[1]. *Kèna*=(by whom?). *ishitâm*=(desired). *imâm vâcham*=this speech *i.e.*, articulate sounds. *vadanti* *i. e.*, people utter. Similarly, the fourth *pâda* means 'Which power is it that directs or induces the eye and the ear to reach their respective objects?'

---

15. See Praṣna Upanishad ii.

The Teacher replies to his worthy disciple who has thus questioned him (as follows)—'Hear what you want—viz. what power directs the several senses such as the mind towards their respective objects and how it directs'.—

2. Because it is the ear of ear, the mind of mind, the speech also of speech, the breath of breath, and the eye of eye, wise men giving up (the ordinary wrong notions) and departing from this world, become immortal.

Srôtra is that by which one hears *i. e.*, the means of hearing sound,—the organ of hearing which reveals sound. *ṣrôtrasya* = of such ear. *ṣrôtram* = ear. It means—that which you ask is 'the ear of ear'. The reply (it may be thought) should properly have been in the form 'So and so, of such and such description, directs the ear etc.' Is it not therefore inappropriate to state in reply (to the disciple's question)—'It is the ear of ear &c.'? (We say that) there is no such impropriety for nobody knows how that (power) can otherwise be characterised. If the prompter of the ear &c., were known to possess a function of its own, apart from that of the ear and so forth, as in the case of a person that uses a scythe, for instance, then this would be an inappropriate reply. But no such entity prompting the ear and the like is known through a distinctive function of its own, as in the case of a mower. It is, on the other hand (only indirectly) known from the activity, such as seeing, desiring and deciding, of the aggregates like the ear, intended to bring about a result, thus—There should be something distinct from the ear and the like for whose sake operates this group of the ear and the rest, as in the case of a house (which is built for a dweller). The existence of something influencing the ear &c., is thus only inferentially known—all aggregates being for the sake of something distinct (from themselves). Hence [1] the reply given by the teacher —viz., that it is the ear of ear and so on— is quite apt. What then do the expressions— 'the ear of ear' &c.,—signify? There is (apparently) no use of one ear to another, just as there is none of one light for another. This is no difficulty, for the following is the significance (of the expressions in the text). The ear, for instance, is known to be capable of making manifest its objects. This

1. All aggregates serving a definite purpose contain an implicit reference to an enjoyer outside of them; for, otherwise, the aggregates would be inexplicable. *Samhatânâm parârthatvam.*

capability of the ear to manifest its objects, arises if the sentient illuminating Self,—eternal, detached and the inmost of all,—subsists and not when it does not. Hence the suitability of the reply given. Compare other *Vedic* texts (of similar import)—'It endures by its own light'; 'All this shines through its light' (*Mund Up*: ii. ii. 10); 'Kindled by whose light, the sun burns' &c. We have in the *Bhagavadgītā* also—'Whatever light in the sun makes the whole word shine &c' (xv, 12); 'O, *Bharata* thus does the Self illumine the whole body' (xiii 33). In the *Kaṭhópanishad* (ii. ii. 13) also we read—'The one eternal of all eternal things, the one sentient principle in all &c.' The ordinary belief is that the ear and the like are themselves the sentient Self. This (misconception) is here removed and (the teacher's) reply—that there is something that can be comprehended (only) by the wise, and which is the inmost of all, constant, unborn, undecaying, immortal, fearless, and which, in respect of the ear &c., is the source of their functions[1]—is, in its content as well as in its form, quite appropriate. Similarly it is the mind of mind—the internal sense. The mind would indeed be incapable of its functions—desiring and deciding—apart from the light of the

17. I read *ṣrótrâdisâmarthyanimittam* instead of *ṣrotrâdi tatsâmarthyanimittam*.

sentient Self. Hence it (the mind) is said to be the mind of mind. Here *manas* and *buddhi*[1] are taken as one, and denoted by the single word *manas*. *yat vâchô ha vâcham*. *yat* means 'since' and should be taken along with each of (the statements)—'the ear of ear' &c. The meaning is consequently—'Since it is the ear of ear, since it is the mind of mind' and so on. In the present statement the accusative *vâcham* should be altered into the nominative (*vâk*) seeing (we have in the next clause) *prâṇasya prâṇaḥ*. Why should not the nominative (*prâṇaḥ* in the latter clause itself be altered into the accusative in conformity with what is found in the former. No; this cannot be done for we should follow (what is implied by) a greater number (of words). In the latter (clause) there are two words (*prâṇaḥ* and *saḥ*) in the nominative and, in accordance with this, *vâcham* should be turned into *vâk*. There will thus be, as is but appropriate, conformity with what is numerically greater. Further it is customary, to designate the thing asked about in the nominative. *saḥ i. e.* that which you have questioned about. *prâṇasya*=of the breathing operation. *prâṇaḥ*=(breath). Breath's ability to breathe is due to it (Brahman), for nothing that is not presided over by the Self can possibly breathe. Compare—'Who

1. *Sankalpavikalpâtmakam manaḥ; niśchayâtmikâ buddhiḥ.*

could respire, who could breathe down, if there were not the bliss in the cave?' *(Tait. Up.* ii. 7*)*; 'It leads up breath and brings it down' *(Kaṭh. Up.* ii. ii. 3). It will presently be stated here also— 'That by which *prâṇa* is prompted, know *that* alone to be Brahman' (It may be said that) while speaking of the organs of sense like the ear it is not quite so appropriate to refer to breath or *prâṇa* as to *ghrâṇa*, the organ of smell. Truly so; but it is intended by the text that the mention of *prâṇa* should imply the organ of smell as well. The point to be made known in this section is that *that* is Brahman for whose sake the totality of the senses employ themselves. Similarly it is the eye of eye *(chakshushaḥ chakshuḥ)*. The ability to comprehend form which is found in the eye,—the perceiver of form,—is conceivabe only when that organ is presided over by the Self. Therefore it is (termed) 'the eye of eye.' Since a questioner desires to *know* that which he questions about, we have to supply here the word, *jnâtvâ* (having known) *i. e.*, having known Brahman which is, as described above, the ear of ear &c. (A further indication that this word should be supplied) is the mention (in the last *pâda*) of the result as being immortality. Immortality is attained through knowledge only. The statement 'having known and given up' means 'having given up in entirety the senses like the ear'. Mistaking the ear and the like for the Self, one is born subject to their limitation,—conditioned by them—and dies and thus eternally transmigrates. Hence (the meaning is)—'knowing that the Self is Brahman, the ear of ear &c. and giving up wrong beliefs such as identifying the Self with the ear &c.' Those who discard this mistaken notion about the ear &c. being the Self are indeed wise men for without the highest wisdom the giving up of such misconceptions is impossible. *prètya* = turning away. *asmât*=from this. *lòkât i. e*, selfish interests relating to sons, friends, wife and relations. In other words, it means 'renouncing all kinds of desires'. *amṛitâ bhavanti* = become endowed with immortality. Compare—'Not by *karma*, not by offspring, not by wealth, but by renunciation only have a few attained immortality'; 'The self-existent ruined the senses &c' (*Kaṭh*: *Up*: ii, i, 1); 'When all the heart's desires are relinquished, then mortal man becomes immortal and enjoys liberation here' (*Id.* ii, iii, 14). Or we may interpret '*asmât lokât prêtya* as 'going away from this body' *i. e.* 'dying', since *atimuchya* by itself may be taken to signify renunciation of desires.[1]

1. The first interpretation, refers to a knower who ceases to feel attachment to anything in the world, including his body, but who continues to live on this earth as his *prârabdha karma* that gave rise to his present life has not yet exhausted itself by bearing fruit. This state is known as *jîvanmukti*. The second interpretation refers to

3. Not there the eye goes: nor speech goes; nor mind. We do not know; neither do we understand how any one can teach it.

As Brahman is the ear of ear &c., *i.e.*, the Self of everything, the eye (*chakshuḥ*) does not reach (*na gachchati*) thither (*tatra*). For motion towards one's own self is impossible. Similarly speech does not go (there). Speech is said to *reach* what it expresses (or its object) when it is uttered by the organ of speech and its meaning is made manifest. Brahman being the Self of that word, as also of the organ which utters it, speech does not reach (thither) just as fire while it burns and illumines (other things) does neither burn itself nor illumine itself.[1] Neither does mind go there. Mind in the same manner desires or decides its objects which are other than itself but cannot desire or decide its own self; and Brahman constitutes that self. Knowledge of a thing arises through the senses or the mind and because Brahman is not reached by either of these,

---

a knower attaining what is termed *vidéhamukti*—complete liberation—which results when a *jîvanmukta* relinquishes his body.

1. I. *e.*, as an object (*vishayatayá*) requiring illumination from outside.

we do not know of what nature it is. We are consequently unable to understand by what means any one can explain that Brahman to a disciple. Such is the sense of the passage. Whatever is perceivable by the senses, *that*, it is possible to indicate to others by genus, quality, function or relationship.[1] Brahman does not possess any of these differentia. Hence the difficulty in explaining its nature to disciples. The need is thus implied for special effort being made in teaching as well as in understanding (the subject).

Since the second half of the *mantra* may be taken to imply the absolute denial of all means of instruction (in respect of Brahman) the following statement is made to repudiate such implication. It is true that it is thus impossible to make another understand Brahman by means of evidence such as sense-perception, but it is quite possible to indicate its nature through *Sâstra*. With this view is cited the following text—

4. 'It is verily other than the known and beyond the unknown.' So have we heard from the ancients who taught us that.

---

1. The following are, in order, the illustrative examples given in the *tikâ*— (i) This is a *Brâhmana*. (ii) He is dark. (iii) This is one that cooks. (iv) He is the king's servant.

Anyat eva=quite different. *tat*=(that) *i.e.*, the entity in question, which has been declared to be the ear of ear &c., and which is beyond their reach. *viditât*=from the known. It is, indeed, other than the known, (for) that is the known which is the direct object of knowing. Everything being known to some one or other, in some place or other, the whole of the manifest (Universe) may certainly be (classed under) 'the known'. The purport is that (Brahman) is different from the Universe. This may imply that, Brahman is then unknown (*avidita*); hence the text adds—*atho aviditât adhi*. *atho*=and. *aviditât*= from the reverse of the known *i. e.*, the unmanifest, *viz.* nescience, the source of the manifest. *adhi*= above; here it means secondarily, 'different'; for, as all know, whatever is above a thing is different from it. That which is known, being finite, mortal and of the nature of sorrow is to be shunned. Declaring Brahman to be other than the known thus means that it is other than what has to be shunned. Similarly declaring it to be other than the unknown amounts to saying that it is other than what may be acquired. It is for the sake of an effect that a cause which is different from it is sought by one that is different (from both). Hence as the individual Self is distinct from the means a well as the end,[1] the expression 'other than the known and the unknown', by declaring that Brahman is distinct from what may be shunned or acquired, identifies it with the individual Self and thus satisfies the desire of the disciple to know Brahman. Nothing but one's own self can in reality[2] be different from both the known and the unknown.[3] Thus the import of the ancient text is that the Self is Brahman. Compare other *Vedic* texts also—'This Self is Brahman' (*Br. Up.* II, v, 19); 'Which Self is untouched by sin' (*Ch: Up:* VIII, vii, 1); 'Which is immediate and primal—which Self is inmost of all' (*Br: Up:* III, iv, 1). It is now stated that the text[4] which thus declares that the Self of all, devoid of all distinctions, whose light is that of pure sentiency, is Brahman, has been handed down traditionally. (It is intended that)

---

1. The text of the *bhâshya* has probably become somewhat corrupt. Two readings are found in Mss. and printed books—one of them, as in the present edition, with only one *na* before *vêdituḥ* or *bhavati*, and the other, as in the Calcutta and Madras editions, with a *na* before both *vêdituh* and *bhavati*. The omission of both the *na's*, appears to yield the best sense; but for such emendation there is not the authority of either of the two Mss. consulted in this translation.

2. I read *vastutaḥ* for *vastunaḥ*.

3. This statement presupposes a division of all entities into three classes—(i) *viditaḥ* (ii) *aviditaḥ* and (iii) *vêditri*.

4. I read *vâkyasya* instead of *vâkyârthasya*.

Brahman should consequently be understood through the traditional teaching of preceptors and not by (oneself) reasoning (merely); nor by disquisition, mental power, learning, austerities, sacrifice and the like. *iti*=thus. *ṣuṣruma*=we have heard. *pûrvêshâm i.e.*, the statement of ancient teachers. *yê*=which teachers. *naḥ*=to us. *tat*= Brahman. *vyâchachakshirê*=explained or taught well.

5. That which is not expressed by words, but through which words are expressed; *that* verily, know thou, is Brahman: it is not what (people) here worship.

When in the first half of the previous *mantra*, it was taught that the Self is Brahman, a doubt occurred to the hearer—'How can the Self be Brahman? The Self is what is charged with the performance of *karma* and *upâsanâ*. Practising, during life, *kârma* or *upâsanâ* as an aid, it seeks to attain heaven or the position of gods such as that of *Brahmâ*. Being the object of *upâsanâ* Brahman must be other than the Self—viz, *Vishnu*, *Iṣvara*, *Indra*, or *Prâṇa*; but it can, under no circumstances, be the Self; for that is contrary to the common sense of mankind. As rationalists say that the Self is different from the Lord, so ritualists (also) worship deities other than the Self (as indicated by statements like) 'Sacrifice for such an one; sacrifice for such an one'. It is therefore to be concluded that Brahman is what is the object of worship and is thus *known* and that the worshipper is altogether distinct from it[1].' (The teacher) perceiving such a doubt from the (facial) expression of the disciple or (perhaps knowing it) from his statements, says—'Do not doubt thus'. *Yat* i. e., which exists as mere sentiency. *vâchâ*—*vâk* is the sensory organ producing sounds, presided over by *Agni* and located in eight places[2] such as the root of the tongue. It may also mean the syllables themselves, certain numbers of which placed in certain orders become definite signs (for conveying) certain meanings. Or the whole word itself considered as sound and suggested by these (separate syllables) may be termed *vâk*[3].

---

1. The gist of the disciple's argument here is that the teaching of the previous *mantra*, viz. that the Self is Brahman, contradicts not merely the common belief of mankind but also heterodox and orthodox systems of philosophy like the *Nyâya* or the *Mîmâmsâ*.

2. *ashtau sthânâni varnânâm urah kanthah sirastathá . jihvâmulam cha dantâscha nâsikoshthau cha tâlu cha.* ‖.

3. Having first interpreted *vâk* as the organ of speech, the commentator proceeds to give the other meaning of the term—'the manifested sound'. Here again there are two views both of which are recounted in the commentary.

Compare—'The syllable *a* is indeed all speech. and this speech, being manifested through mutes, semi-vowels and sibilants, becomes manifold and differentiates itself into various forms'[1]. *vâchâ i.e.*, by that which becomes determined as words and is dependent (for its production) on the organs of speech and of which all this—metre, prose, song; truth and falsehood; are only varieties. *anabhyud-itam*=not made known or not expressed. *yèna i.e.*, by which Brahman. *vâk abhyudyate i.e.*, speech together with its sensory organ is made known or used by the sentient light in the sense to be conveyed. Compare what has already been stated—'Which is the speech of speech'—as also passages like the following in the *Bṛhadâraṇyakôpanishad*—'When speaking, speech' (I, iv, 7); 'Who controls speech from inside' (III, vii, 17). Again (elsewhere) having raised a question thus—'That speech which is in man is placed in sounds. Has any *Brâhmaṇa* understood it?', the reply is given—'That is speech by which (one) speaks in a dream'. That is the (true) speech of the speaker, eternal and of the nature of the sentient light. Compare—

Some thinkers hold that the *varṇas* themselves are the word and that the sense is conveyed directly through them. Others maintain that the word is different from the *varṇas* and is revealed by them. This word is eternal in its nature and is known as *sphôta* and through suggesting the *sphôta*, it is said, the *varṇas* convey the meaning only indirectly.

1. I read *saishā* for *saishâsya*.

'The speech of the speaker can never disappear' (*Br. Up.* IV, iii, 26). *tat eva i.e.* the Self only. *Brahma i.e.* the supreme, known as the Infinite. It is called '*Brahman*' being great (from the root *bṛh.* 'to grow'). *viddhi*=know. The significance of *eva* is as follows—Having discarded all definitions of what is really indefinable, distinctionless, supreme and harmonious, through limiting adjuncts like speech—such as, 'the speech of speech', 'the eye of eye' and so forth, 'the agent, enjoyer, knower, controller and ruler', 'Brahman is knowledge, is bliss'—know that the Self only is Brahman. *na idam Brahma*=(not this the Brahman). *yat idam i.e.* the conditioned, such as *Îsvara* (conceived as) different from the Self. *upâsate*=worship. Though it has already been stated 'That verily, know thou, is Brahman,' the fourth *pâda* adds that whatever is not Self is not Brahman for the sake of emphasis or for repudiating the belief that anything but the Self could be Brahman.

6. That which is not thought by the mind, but by which, they say, the mind is thought; *that* verily, know thou, is Brahman ; it is not what (people) here worship.

Manas is the internal sense and is (here) used to signify both the *buddhi* and *manas*. *Manas* is that which thinks and is the common factor in all sensory (operations), being related to all kinds of objects. It is characterised by desire &c. as recorded in—'Desire, decision, doubt, faith, want of faith, boldness, cowardice, shame, intellect, fear, —all this is only mind.' (*Br. Up.* I, v, 3). *manasâ*=(by means of such mind). *Yat i.e.* the light of intelligence, which is the illuminator of the mind, because Brahman is its controller, being the source of its light. *na manute i.e.* one does not decide or desire. The Self being the in-most of all objects, the mind cannot move towards it (which is its own self). (Rather) the mind itself is able to think only when it is illumined by the light of intelligence residing inside. Therefore, it is, that knowers of Brahman declare that the mind with all its functions is thought or pervaded by Brahman. Hence one should know that the Self of the mind, the internal cogniser, only is Brahman. The fourth *pâda* is to be understood as before.

7. That which is not seen by the eye, but by which eyes are seen; *that* verily, know thou, is Brahman; it is not what (people) here worship.

Chakshushá=by the eye operating with (the aid of) mind. *na paşyati i. e.* one does not perceive. *chakshúmshi i.e.* the operations of the eye as distinguished from those of the mind. *paşyati*=knows or pervades, through its inherent light of intelligence. The rest (of the *mantra* should be understood) as before.

8. That which is not heard by the ear but by which ears are heard; *that* verily, know thou, is Brahman; it is not what (people) here worship.

Srótram, a transformation of space, presided over by the deities of space and acting in conjunction with the mind. The rest (to be understood) as before.

9. That which is not breathed by *prána* but through which *prana* breathes; *that* verily, know thou, is Brahman; it is not what (people) here worship.

Práṇa=ghráṇa=the organ of smell, a transformation of elemental earth, located in the nostrils and acting conjointly with breath and mind. *na práṇiti*=does not perceive, as for instance, (it does), odour. The rest (to be understood) as before.

End of the First Section.

SECOND SECTION.

1. If thou thinkest that thou hast understood (Brahman) well, thou knowest it but in a small (form), whether it refer (to the individualisd Self) or to gods; and thou, I think, hast yet to investigate (it).—I think I understand.

Lest the disciple who has been taught that he (himself) is Brahman, the reverse of what can be shunned or acquired, should think 'I know well; I myself am Brahman', the teacher states as above and (desires to) test the pupil's knowledge. Should not clear conviction in the pupil that he has understood well, be welcome to the teacher? True, clear conviction is welcome; but not in the form 'I know (Brahman) well' for it is possible to *know* only that which can be an object of consciousness, as, for instance, in the case of burning a thing that can be burnt by the burning fire; but not the nature of fire itself. The final import of all the Upanishads is that the Self of all the knowers is Brahman. Here also the same has been set forth in the form of an answer to a question in i, 2. and specially affirmed in i, 5. The traditional faith of knowers of Brahman has been indicated in i, 4 and the topic will hereafter be concluded (in the same strain) in ii, 3. Thus it is but right to remove from (the mind of) the disciple (the idea) that he knows Brahman well. Certainly the knowing principle in the knower cannot be known as the burning principle in fire cannot be burnt. Nor indeed is there a knower, other than Brahman, to whom it may become an object of consciousness. The text—'There is no knower other than that '(Br: Up: III, viii, 11) denies a second knower, from which (we may conclude that) the belief that Brahman is *known* is altogether illusory. The teacher is thus right in stating as above.

Yadi=if ever. *manyasê*=(you think). *su vêda iti* i.e., 'I know Brahman very well'. (The teacher) speaks thus conditionally because an intelligent pupil, whose sins are at an end, does comprehend what is taught, though it be difficult of comprehension; while another (who is dull) does not. It is also known that as recounted in *Ch.Up*: (VII, v) the learned *Virôchana,* the lord of *asuras* and son of *Prajâpati,* when taught the nature of the Self, owing to his inherent sin, thought that the body was the Self, although such a view was untenable, being the very opposite of what was meant. Again *Indra*, the lord of gods, unable to comprehend the same when taught once, twice and a third time understood correctly what was meant from the very beginning only on the fourth occasion—thus biding (his time for) the removal of his original deficiency. In our experience also, though taught by the same teacher, some understand rightly, some wrongly, some differently and others not at all. What shall we say (of the present subject)—the entity of Self which is supersensuous! There is in respect of this subject great divergence (of opinion) among enquirers—some saying 'It exists'; others 'It does not'. Thus—because it is difficult of comprehension—the teacher is right in speaking conditionally with an 'if', although the disciple has, after due reflection, declared that he has understood Brahman. *dabhram*=small. *eva* = (quite). *api*= (and). *nûnam*= (indeed). *tvam*=(you). *vèttha*= know. *Brahmaṇaḥ*=of Brahman. *rûpam*=form. Are there many forms of Brahman—some small, others great—that you say 'quite small?' Yes; many indeed are the forms of Brahman resulting from the limitations of name and form; but in itself (Brahman) is not so. In itself, it is devoid of all forms, as also of sound and so forth as recorded in *Kaṭhôpanishad* (I, iii, 15)—'Devoid of sound, of touch, of form; imperishable; so also is it—the eternal—without flavour or odour?'

Well, since that by which a thing is defined forms its essence, that by which Brahman is defined must constitute its essence. Hence we may say that *chaitanya* or sentiency, which is not the essence of any of the elements like earth, or of their transformations—taken individually or in totality—or either of the organs of sense like the ear and the inner sense, constitutes the nature or essence of Brahman, and that Brahman is accordingly characterised by sentiency. There are also *Vedic* texts (favouring such a view). Compare—'Brahman is *knowledge*, bliss' (*Br*: *Up*.III ix, 8); 'Wholly solid *sentiency*' (*Br*. *Up*. II, iv 12): '*Intelligence* is Brahman' (*Ait*: *Up* v, 3); 'Existence, *sentiency*, infinite is Brahman (Tait: Up: II, i, 1)—all of which describe Brahman (in terms of sentiency). Truly so; but even there Brahman is defined as sentiency and so forth, through its limiting adjuncts viz., the mind, the body and the various organs of sense, for (Brahman) reflects their (characteristics) in their growth, contraction, suspense, destruction and so on; but, in itself, it does not (undergo any change whatever), and is, as will hereafter be established, 'unknown to the knower and known only to those that do not know it.' *yat*=which. *asya* *i.e.* of this. These words are to be taken with *brahmaṇô rûpam*. It is not merely what you know of Brahman in its form of the individualised Self that is small; but also what you know of Brahman in its divine form. Thus I think. Whatever is human or divine is limited by adjuncts and is not thus different from smallness or finitude. But *that* Brahman which shakes off all adjuncts, is peaceful, endless, one without a second, known as *bhûman* (that which is much) and eternal, is not at all an object of knowledge. This is the purport of the passage. Hence I think (*manye*) that even now it (Brahman) remains to be investigated (*mîmâmsyam*) by you (*té*). The disciple, thus addressed by the teacher. sitting in a solitary place and concentrating his thoughts, pondered over the meaning of the text quoted by the teacher and having come to a decision through reasoning and intuitive experience, approached the teacher and said—*manye viditam* i. e. 'I think that Brahman is now understood by me'. How? Pray, listen—

2. I do not at all think I know well; nor that I do not know; but know too. And he among us knows it who knows this—'Not that I do not know; but know too'.

The first *pâda* means—'I do not at all think I know Brahman well'. The second *pâda* meaning 'I do certainly know, is[1] in answer to the

1. I read *védaiveti* in place of *védacheti*.

objection, viz. 'You do not in that case understand Brahman'. By the force of *cha* (after *vèda* we have to understand) *na vèda cha* (i. e. 'I do not know either). Does not all this involve a contradiction? If you think you do not know well, how can you say you know also? If you, on the other hand, think you know, how is it you do not think you know well? When a thing is known by one, it is a self-contradiction to say that the same is not known, unless it be a case of doubt or delusion. Brahman, to be sure, it cannot be held, is to be known doubtfully or wrongly for doubt and error are everywhere known to cause only evil. The pupil, though thus shaken (in his belief) by the teacher, did not waver owing to the influence of the traditional teaching imparted to him in i, 4, and of his reasoned and intuitive conviction, but thundered forth evincing his firm belief in the knowledge of Brahman. How? As follows—*yo nastadveda tadveda no na vedeti veda-cha*. *Yaḥ*=whoever. *naḥ*=among us, fellow students. *tat* i. e., the above statement. *vèda*=understands rightly. *tat*=(Brahman). *vèda*=(knows). What is that statement? The fourth *pâda* furnishes the answer. (The disciple) here repeats—as confirmed by reason and intuitive perception—what was stated by the teacher in the first half of i, 4, (but) in different words so that it may fall in with the view of the teacher and thus remove from his mind any mistaken idea that the disciple is dull. The disciple is thus justified in proclaiming as he did.

Dropping the form of a dialogue between the teacher and his disciple, the *Sruti* now inculcates[1] directly what forms the essence of the whole of the preceding conversation—

3. To whomsoever it is not known, to him it is known; to whomsoever it is known, he does not know. Unknown to knowers and known (only) to those that do not know.

Yasya=to a knower of Brahman. *amatam*= not known i.e., whose conviction is that Brahman is not an object of knowledge. *tasya*=to such a knower. *matam* i. e., Brahman is clear. *matam yasya na véda saḥ* i. e., whoever, on the other hand, believes that he apprehends Brahman, does not at all understand (the nature of Brahman). (The second half of the *mantra*) merely reaffirms these statements relating to knowers and the ignorant. *avijnátam*=unknown i. e., Brahman is not an object of knowledge. *vijánatam*=to true knowers.

1. I read *arthamavabódhayati* instead of *arthaméva bódhayati.*

vijnâtam=known (i.e. is an object of knowledge.) *avijanâtam*=to those that do not know properly. The word (*avijânatâm*) refers only to such as mistake the senses, mind or intellect for the Self and not to the absolutely uncultured, for the latter never feel that they have understood Brahman. In the case of those, however, that mistake adjuncts like the senses, mind or intellect, for the Self, the delusion that Brahman is apprehended by them is quite possible, because they do not perceive the distinction between Brahman and its adjuncts, which are clearly knowable. The statement in *pâda* 4 is for indicating the *prima facie* view. Or, the second half (in its entirety) may be viewed as assigning a reason (for what has been stated in the first half.)[1]

It has been declared that (Brahman) is not known to knowers. If Brahman be thus totally unknown to them, there will then be no distinction whatever between ordinary persons and knowers.

1. To take the ordinary illustration of a person mistaking mother-of-pearl for silver. To one that knows it is mother-of-pearl the superimposed silver does not at all appear; but to one that is ignorant of its real nature, the superimposed idea occurs. Stating the same in general terms, —those that know the 'reality' do not perceive the 'appearance' and those who perceive the 'appearance' do not know the 'reality'. Similarly in the present case also where *jnâtatva* or 'being known as an object' is superimposed upon Brahman and does not in reality pertain to its nature.

Further, the statement 'unknown to knowers' is self-contradictory. How then can such Brahman be understood properly? In answer to such a question, is said—

4. (When Brahman) is known through every state of consciousness, (it then) is rightly known; for (by such knowledge) one attains immortality. Through one's own self doth real power come; and through self-knowledge comes immortality.

Prati bódha viditam means 'perceived in every state of consciousness'. The word *bódha* refers to 'mental states'. The Self to which all mental states become objects of knowledge is known through every one of those states.[1] The witness of all mental operations, whose essence is mere sentiency, is implied by those operations themselves as being the common element of them all. There is no other means of knowing the inner Self. Hence the meaning is that when Brahman is known as the inmost essence of mental perceptions, then, that is *matam* or right knowledge. When once

1. As heat, for instance, is known through every heated object.

Brahman is admitted to be the witness of all mental perceptions, it follows, that it is of the nature of sentiency, without beginning or end, eternal, pure in form, identical with oneself, devoid of distinctions and one in all beings, for there is no distinguishing feature (between one such witness and another)—as in the case of space for instance (encompassed by) a jar or a mountain cave. Thus the teaching of the *Vèdic* text that Brahman is different from the known as well as from the unknown is summarised here as referring to the unqualified (higher Brahman). Compare another *Vèdic* text—'The seer of sight, hearer of hearing, thinker of thought, knower of knowledge'.

When, however, *pratibòdhaviditam* is interpreted as 'known by the characteristic act of knowing', on the supposition that Brahman is the agent in the act of knowing and that the agent is known through his action, *viz.*, knowing, as for instance, in the case of the wind which may be indicated by its shaking the branches of trees, the Self becomes a mere substance possessing the faculty of knowing and not knowledge itself. Knowledge (only) appears and disappears in it. When knowledge appears, the Self becomes distinguishable by the act of knowing; when knowledge disappears, then, being dissociated from knowing, it becomes a mere (unintelligent) substance. Hence it will (in this view) be impossible to get over the objection that Brahman is changeable, composed of parts, transient, impure and so on.

According to the followers of *Kanâda*, however, knowledge arises from contact of the Self with the mind and inheres (as a quality) in the Self, which is consequently spoken of as a 'knower'. Thus the Self does not change (through knowing as in the previous view). Being a substance (it becomes endowed with the attribute of knowledge,) as a jar becomes associated with its particular colour (when it comes in cantact with fire).[1] This view also makes Brahman a mere substance, devoid of intelligence and contradicts texts like—'Brahman is knowledge, bliss' (*Br. Up*: III ix 8); 'Intelligence is Brahman' (*Ait. Up*. v. 3). Further (the mind cannot come into contact with the Self) as it is without parts and has consequently no surface (where contact may take place). (If contact be

---

1. The distinction between the two views here criticised should be noticed. According to the first view, knowledge is an *act* and the Self is what *knows*; according to the second, knowledge is a *quality* and inheres, like all qualities, in the Self, but requires for its manifestation the previous contact of the Self with the mind. The *siddhânta* view also makes *jnâna* an act or *kriyâ* but it is only what is termed *vritti jnâna* or ordinary mental perception. Thus only the mind becomes changeable through the act of knowing but not the Self. What constitutes the essence of the Self—*svarûpa jnâna*—is neither an act, nor a quality. It is eternal and subsists in itself. 'The soul is not a knower, but knowledge; not intelligent, but intelligence.'

inferred from the fact that the Self is pervading and) is therefore in intimate union (with everything)[1], it will be impossible to maintain that remembrance can (as is admitted by all) arise only under definite conditions.[2] It would, moreover, by making the Self susceptible of attachment, clash with statements in the *srutis* and *smṛitis* and with reason as well. Compare—'Being unattached it does not cling (to any thing)' (*Br. Up*: III, ix, 26) 'Unattached and yet holding all' (*Bh. Gi.* xiii, 14). As for reason. Only a thing with attributes can combine with another—also possessing attributes;

1. This sentence is highly elliptical and the interpretation given by the *ṭikākāra* has been followed in translating it. A semi-colon may, for the sake of clearness, be placed after *pradesâbhâvât*.

2. The fact admitted by all, to which reference is made here, is that remembrance of a thing is only after it has been perceived. The position of the opponent is this—Being *vibhu*, the Self is in eternal union with all things and so with mind as well. It cannot therefore be maintained that the Self will not come into contact with the mind because it does not present a surface where contact may take place. This position is refuted as follows—If the Self be always in intimate union with the mind, objects should be remembered not merely after perception but during perception as well, when also the required conditions—the union of the mind with the Self and the reviving cause which, in the present case, is the object itself—exist. Such a conclusion is subversive of the fundamental notions about the difference between perception and memory.

but not with what is dissimilar. Hence it is against reason (to hold) that what is unqualified, devoid of distinction, different from everything, unites or comes into contact with anything of a different nature. Thus the conclusion that Brahman is the Self, eternal and of the nature of never-disappearing intelligence, can be established only when the Self is identical with the witness of all perceptions and not otherwise. Therefore the meaning of *pratibôdhaviditam* is as we have explained.

Again, if *pratibôdhaviditam* be explained as referring to 'knowing by one's own self', (we have to say that) such an explanation is applicable only to the conditioned Self, distinguished, on account of its adjunct viz. the mind, from the pure Self, as in—'He discovers the Self in himself' (*Ch: Up*: IV iv, 23); 'Thou, best of men, know thyself in thyself' (*Bh. Gi.* x, 15) &c. If, on the other hand, the Self is (taken as) unconditioned and therefore one, it can neither be known by itself nor by anything else. Moreover, being itself sentiency, (the Self) does not need another sentient principle (to know itself), just as one light does not stand in need of another light.

If we understand Self-consciousness in the Buddhistic sense, knowledge becomes momentary and the (continuous principle of the) Self is eliminated,[1] which again contradicts texts like, 'There is no disappearance of the knowledge of the knower, because it always persists' (*Br. Up*: IV, iii, 30); 'Eternal, mighty and pervading' (*Mund: Up:* I. 6); 'That indeed is the great unborn Self, undecaying, undying, immortal, and fearless' (*Br. Up*: IV. iv, 25).

As regards the interpretation by others of *pratibôdhaviditam* as causeless or intrinsic knowledge[2], as in deep sleep[3] or sudden enlighten-

---

1. If we grant that knowledge perceives itself, then since perception can refer only to what exists in the present moment, knowledge in one moment cannot perceive knowledge in the next moment. There being thus no continuous perception of knowledge, it becomes momentary, as indeed every thing is according to the school of Buddhistic phiolosophers here referred to (*vainâṣikâs*). Again, when we grant that knowledge is self-perceiving, there will be no need to postulate, as is done in the *Vêdânta*, the existence of a *sâkshî* or a persisting witness of all mental notions and the continuous principle of the Self thus becomes eliminated from the system.

2. According to this interpretation *pratibôdha* means what is familiar to students of *Yôga* as *asamprajnâtasamâdhi* which ranks higher than *samprajnâtasamâdhi* or conscious *samâdhi*. It is pure absorption which restores to Selfhood the devotee who has gradually released himself from all the trammels of the *upâdhis* inclusive of the mind.

3. The happiness of perfect tranquility experienced during sleep is stated to be the result of such intrinsic intelligence, the same not being attributable to any extraneous cause.

ment[1], (we have to state that) whether knowledge be intrinsic or extrinsic, sudden or recurring—it (the Self) is still what is known through a state of consciousness.[2] *amritatvam*=deathlessness *i.e.* abiding in one's own self, liberation. *hi*=because. *vindaté*=obtains. That is, since (liberation is attained by means of) what is known through states of consciousness, what is so known is assuredly rightly known. The Self is the inmost essence of a notion[3] and knowledge relating to the Self is the cause of immortality. Becoming what is non-Self can never be said to form immortality and since immortality is but being one's own self it cannot be caused by anything extraneous. Similarly mortality for the Self is due to mistaking it, from nescience, for what is different from it[4].

---

1. When Brahman is realised, the devotee loses his individualised form and, there being thus no scope for any further mental operation, the final perception resulting in *Brahma-realisation* is termed *sakridvijnânam*, which literally means 'knowledge for once.' *Akriyabrahmâtmatvânuabhavé sati pramâtṛtvânupapattau punarjnânâsambhavât, sadyómuktikâraṇam sakridvijnânam pratibodhaḥ.—Tîkâ.*

2. Thus the meaning of the expression as orginally explained is re-affirmed.

3. I read *bódhasya hi pratyak âtmâ; âtmavishayatvam cha amṛtatvé hétuḥ.*

4. The function of true knowledge is merely to remove this mistaken notion—that the Self is something different from what it really is and not to *effect* or *generate móksha* newly.

How then does one attain immortality through such self-knowledge? This question is answered in the second half of the *mantra*. *âtmanâ* =by one's own self. *vindatê*=obtains. *vîryam*= strength or power. Power due to wealth, assistance, incantations, magic herbs, austerities and application cannot overcome death, for it is derived from transient things. The power of self-knowledge, on the other hand, is got through one's own self and not through anything else. Thus—since the power of self-knowledge is derived from nothing extraneous, that power is able to conquer death. Because the power of self-knowledge is got through oneself, it follows that by self-knowledge (*vidyayâ*) immortality (*amṛtatvam*) is attained. The condition laid down for achieving immortality is quite suitable because we find recorded in another *Upanishad* (*Mundaka*)—'This Self is not to be reached by one devoid of strength' (III, ii, 4)[1].

5. If one should know here, then there is use; if one should not here know (there results) great loss. Hence, seeking (Reality) in all beings, wise men become immortal after death.

1. The strength arising from knowledge is this—that one is in reality absolutely free—and the consequent sense of security leads one to the happiness of peace.

To experience—through nescience—birth, decay, death, disease and so on in the form of beings —whether as gods or men or beasts or manes—all thick with the sorrows of life—is indeed a misery. If (*chêt*) one that is qualified and capable knew (*avèdît*) the Self in this human life (*iha*), then (*atha*) there would be permanence, utility, goodness or reality (*satyam*).[1] *Na cha iha avêdît* i.e. if one, thus qualified, did not find it out in this life. *mahatî vinashtiḥ i.e.*, long or infinite ruin follows, in the form of metempsychosis, characterised by the infinite and unbroken series of birth, decay and death. Thus wise *Brâhmanas* (*dhîrâḥ*) that can discriminate between good and evil (do as follows) —*bhûtêshu bhûtêshu*=in all beings whether movable or immovable. *vichitya i.e.*, discovering or realising the one Reality of the Self. *dhîrâḥ*=wise men. *prêtya i.e.*, turning back and ceasing to take part in this shadowy life, characterised by *meum* and *tuum* and identifying themselves with the non-

1. To the four meanings of *satyam* given in the commentary, the *tîkâ* adds four more—'birth', 'long life', 'wealth', 'reputation' and states that these also result from *Brahma-knowledge*. The object of mentioning them in the present case, however, is only to glorify that knowledge. The one true result yielded by it and intended to be prominently mentioned here is 'the attainment of Brahmahood itself' and its statement in the *last pâda* of the *mantra* indicates the prominence that is to be given to it in recounting the uses of *Brahma-knowledge*. The other rewards are mentioned here only by the way.

dual, all-encompassing Truth. *ámṛtā bhavanti*= (become immortal) *i.e.* become Brahman itself as recorded in the text—'He who knows the supreme Brahman indeed becomes Brahman itself' (*Mund: Up:* III, ii, 9).

End of the Second Section.

THIRD SECTION.

1. Brahman, it is said, conquered (once) for the gods and the gods gloried in that conquest of Brahman. They thought—'Ours is this victory, and ours alone, this greatness.'

Whatever *is*, is known, through (one or other of the instruments of knowledge; whatever *is not*, is not known and is absolute nothing as, for example, a hare's horn. And Brahman, because it is not known, should also be nothing. Lest the dull-witted, hearing what has been stated in the second half of ii, 3, delude themselves thus, the following episode is narrated. It is this same Brahman which controls (all) in all respects, which is god higher than all gods, the over-lord of all lords, incomprehensible, the source of victory for the gods and of defeat for the demons. How can it be nothing? The subsequent passages contain sentiments favouring such a view. Or (it may be understood as) glorifying self-knowledge. How? Through self-knowledge did divine *Agni* and others attain pre-eminence among gods and *Indra*, greater (pre-eminence) still. Or again (we may say that) the episode shows how difficult it is to comprehend Brahman. Thus with much difficulty did *Agni* and others—the very mightiest—know Brahman. Similarly *Indra* also, the king of the gods. Or (we may understand that) the whole (episode) is (narrated) in reference to the injunction (to contemplate Brahman) as hereinafter given (in iv, 6)[1] or the episode (may be viewed as) pointing out—in contrast to Brahma-knowledge—that the ordinary belief of beings that they are agents, enjoyers and so forth is but illusory, like the belief of the gods in respect of their victory.

Brahman i. e., the Supreme described above. *ha*=it is said. *dévèbhyah*=for the sake of gods. *vijigyè*=conquered. In the strife between the gods and the demons, (Brahman) vanquishing the demons, the enemies of the world and breakers of the divine law, transferred to the gods its victory together with its results, for the stability of the world. *tasya Brahmanaḥ*=of that Brahman. *ha*. (This is for emphasis merely). *vijayè*=in (victory). *dévâḥ*=(gods) such as *Agni*. *amahíyanta*=became

1. According to the *ṭíkâkâra*, this is the explanation most acceptable to the commentator, since in what follows in section iv, there is found a specific injunction to meditate upon Brahman. The other explanations are suggested as being only possible.

great. *tê i. e.* those gods, not realising then that the victory and glory were of Brahman who abides in themselves as their inner Self, the Lord, omniscient, the bestower of all fruits of *karma* to all beings, omnipotent, and desirous of the sustained existence of the Universe. *îkshanta*=thought as follows—*asmâkam êva ayam vijayaḥ*=ours alone, this victory. *asmâkam êva ayam mahimâ*=ours alone, this greatness, achieved by us *Agni* and the rest in our individualised forms. *iti*=thus. We enjoy our positions as *Agni*, *Vâyu*, *Indra* and so on in virtue of our victory. This is not due to the Lord residing in us.

2. They say, it understood that (feeling of the gods) and appeared before them ; (but) they did not know what the venerable Being was.

Tat=Brahman. *ha*=it is said. *êshâm i.e.*, of gods who were thus feeling falsely. For Brahman is the witness of all beings, the propelling power of all their organs of sense. Knowing this false belief of the gods and pitying them, lest they also, like the demons, meet with defeat in consequence of their false pride and desiring to favour them by removing that pride, it appeared (*prâdurbabhûva*) for their good before them (*têbhyaḥ*). That is, it showed itself before their organs of sense in a most mighty and awe-inspiring form created by its great *yògic* power[1], *tat*=Brahman who thus appeared. *na vyajânata* =the gods did not at all understand. *kim*=what? *idam*=this. *yaksham*=adorable (being). *iti*=thus.

3. They said to *Agni* 'O *Játavédas*, find this out—what this venerable Being is.' 'Yes' (he said.)

Tè i.e. the gods who did not understand (what the apparition was), feeling afraid inwardly and wishing to know. *Agnim*=to *Jâtavèdas*, their leader who is practically omniscient. *abruvan*= said. *Jâtavêda*=(O *Agni*). *ètat i.e.*, this Being which has appeared before us. *vijânthi*=find out definitely what it is; for you are the most brilliant among us. *tathâ iti i. e.*, he said 'yes'.

4. He hastened towards it and it said to him 'Who art thou?'. (*Agni*) replied—'I am *Agni* indeed, I am *Játavèdas*.'

---

1. *Yòga* is explained in the *tikâ* as the union of the three fundamental *gunas* of *sattvam*, *rajas* and *tamas* and hence as signifying *mâyâ ṣakti*.

Tat abhyadravat i.e., *Agni* went towards it—the apparition. *tam i. e., Agni* who came near and desired to speak but, being stunned, remained silent before it. *abhyavadat i. e.,* the apparition said—'Who are you?' *(kôstti).* Thus asked by Brahman, *Agni* said *(abravît),* in self-esteem—*Agniḥ vai aham asmi iti; Jâtavêdâ vai aham asmi iti i.e.,* well-famed, as *Agni* and *Jâtavêdas*—by this double name.

5. (The Being asked *Agni*)—'What strength in thee, thus famed?' (*Agni*) replied—'I can burn all this that is on earth.'

Brahman said to him who thus replied—*Tasmin tvayi* i. e., in you thus famed, from name and power. *kim viryam*=what strength? He replied—*idam sarvam*=all this. *dahêyam*=I can turn to ashes. *yat idam* i.e., whatever is—such as immovable things. *pṛthivyâm*=on the earth. *iti*=thus. The word *pṛthivî* is here used in an indicatory sense, for the fire can burn whatever is in the heavens as well.

6. (The Being) placed before him a straw, saying 'Burn this.' (*Agni*) went towards it with all his might, but could not burn it;

and he returned thence and said, 'I have not been able to find out what venerable Being this is.'

Tasmai i. e., before *Agni* so proud. *tṛnam*=straw. *nidadhau* i.e., Brahman placed. It said—*ttat*=this. *daha*=burn. *iti*=thus. Thus told by Brahman and asked by it to give up his false pride that he can burn all, if he failed to burn it, *Agni* went towards it (*tat upapréyáya*) with all enthusiastic pride (*sarvajavêna.*) Having gone (he) did not succeed (*na ṣaṣâka*) in burning (*dagdhum*) it (*tat*). *saḥ* i.e., *Jâtavêdas* who was ashamed because he was unable to burn it and had thus broken his word. *tata èva*=from that Being. *nivavṛté* i. e., returned silently to the gods (saying) 'I have not been able (*na aṣakam*) to know (*vijnâtum*) what the venerable Being is (*kim êtat yaksham iti*).'

7. They said to *Vãyu*—'O *Vãyu*, find this out—what this venerable Being is.' 'Yes', (he said).

8. He hastened towards it and it said to him 'Who art thou ?'. (*Vàyu* replied)—'I am *Vàyu* indeed ; I am *Mátarisvá*.'

9. (The Being asked *Váyu*)—'What strength in thee thus famed ?' (Vâyu) replied—'I can carry all this that is on earth'.

10. (The Being) placed before him a straw saying 'Take it up.' (*Vâyu*) went towards it with all his might but could not take it ; and he returned thence and said 'I have not been able to find out what this venerable Being is—'

Atha=then. *Vâyum*—so called because he blows or carries fragrance with him. *mâtariṣvâ*—one that moves (*ṣvayati*) in the heavens (*mâtari*). *âdadîya*=I can carry. The rest (to be understood) as before.

11. Then they said to *Indra*—'O *Maghavan*, find this out—what this venerable Being is'. 'Yes' he said. He hastened towards it (but) it disappeared from before him.

Indra=the great lord (of gods). *maghavá*—so called because he has many sacrifices(to his credit)[1]. *tásmát* *i. e.*, from *Indra* who had approached it. *tat* i.e. Brahman. *tiròdadhe*=disappeared—to humiliate him the more for his pride, as the lord (of all gods). And *Indra* could not even speak to it.

12. In the same place he met a woman—most beautiful—(*Umá*), the daughter of *Himavàn* and said to her—'What is this venerable Being?'

Tasmin èva ákâse i.e., in the same place where the Being showed itself and disappeared and where *Indra* himself was, at the time of its disappearance. *Indra* stood in the same place wondering what that apparition was and did not return like *Agni* and *Váyu*. Knowledge in the disguise of *Umá* appeared before him, seeing his devotion to the Being (that had appeared.) *saḥ*=*Indra*. *tám* i.e., *Umâ*. *bahusòbhamânâm*=(most beautiful)—Knowledge is surely the most beautiful of all that is beautiful. As applied to knowledge the epithet is very appropriate. *Haimavatîm*=decorated with golden ornaments i.e. beautiful as if decorated with golden ornaments. Or we may

1. I read *yajnavattvât* instead of *balavattvât*.

interpret this as 'daughter of *Himavân*' because *Umâ* is such. *Indra* approached her (with his question) for she being always by the side of the all-knowing Brahman knows it. *tâm* i.e. *Umâ*. *ha*=it is said. *uvâcha* i.e. asked as follows—*kim ètat yaksham iti i.e.* what is this Being which, having shown itself (for a while), has disappeared ?

End of the Third Section.

FOURTH SECTION.

1. She replied—'This is Brahman, to be sure, and you but glory thus, verily, in its victory.' Then only he knew it was Brahman.

She said '*Brahma iti*' i. e. (this is Brahman), *ha*=to be sure. *Brahmaṇaḥ*=of Brahman, the Lord. *vai*=verily. *vijaye*=(in victory). The demons were conquered by Brahman itself and you were but instruments therein. In its victory you glory. *ètat*=(so much)—to be taken with the verb. Your belief— 'ours alone is this victory; ours alone, this greatness' is merely illusory. *tataḥ* i.e., from that reply of *Umá*. *èva*=only. *vidámchakára* i.e. *(Indra)* understood. *Brahma iti*=as Brahman. The emphasis on *tataḥ* (indicated by *èva*) points out (that *Indra* did) not (know it) independently (but only when instructed by some one else).

2. Thence indeed are these gods—*Agni*, *Vàyu* and *Indra*—above other gods, for they, it

was, that touched Brahman closest; for they, it was, that first understood Brahman.

Since these gods—*Agni*, *Vâyu* and *Indra*—went nearest Brahman by conversing with it and seeing it, they (*ètè devâḥ*) therefore (*tasmât*) by their excellences—their happy lot of possessing power and virtue—greatly (*atitarâm*) surpass other gods (*anyân dèvan*). *iva* after *atitarâm* is an expletive merely or (may be taken as) emphatic in its significance. *yadagnirvâyurindraḥ*—viz., *Agni*, *Vâyu* and *Indra*. *tè*=those gods. *hi*=since. *ènat i.e.* Brahman. *nèdishṭham*=nearest, dearest. *pasparṣuḥ*=touched Brahman i.e., through conversation &c., as narrated above. *tè*=they. *hi*=because. *ènat i.e.* Brahman. *prathamaḥ*=*prathamâḥ* =being first or foremost. *vidâmchakâra*=*vidâmchakruḥ*=(understood). *Brahmaṇiti*=as Brahman.

3. Hence indeed is *Indra* more than other gods, for he, it was, that touched it closest; for he, it was, that first understood Brahman.

Agni and *Vâyu* also learnt only from *Indrâ*'s statement, who first heard from *Umâ* that it was Brahman; therefore (*tasmât*) does Indra surpass greatly other gods. The rest has already been explained.

4. This is an illustration of it (Brahman) as relating to its divine form :—as the flashing of lightning ; and the twinkling (of the eye).

Tasya=of Brahman. *eshaḥ*=the following *âdeṣaḥ*=statement of a parallel. By *âdeṣa* is (here) meant the giving of a parallel instance to Brahman who is (really) without a parallel. What is it? *yad ètat* i. e. what is well-known to all. *vidyutaḥ vyadyutat*—This is interpreted as 'the flashing of lightning', for (taking it literally) the expression means 'derived its light from lightning' which however, is inappropriate (in regard to Brahman which is self-luminous). *â* indicates similarity. The expression thus means—'like the flash of lightning', as is also recorded in another text—'Like sudden lightning' (*Br. Up*: II, iii, 6). Brahman showed itself like a lightning to the gods (but) once and disappeared. Or we may supply the word *tèjas* (light) after *vidyutaḥ* and understand by the expression 'flashed like the light of a lightning'. *iti* points to the parallel instance and means 'as'. *it*=and. The following is another parallel (to it). What is it ? *nyamîmishat* i.e. (twinkled) like the eye, (taking the verb) in a non-causative sense. *â* (as before) indicates analogy (only) The meaning is 'also as the opening and the closing of the eye in respect of its object'. *iti*=thus. *adhidaivatam* i.e. a parallel (to the Supreme) in reference to its divine form.[1]

5. Next in regard to the individualised Self—the mind appears to reach Brahman and by the same (mind, one) remembers (Brahman) constantly ; volition (also, likewise).

Atha=then. *adhyâtmam* i,e. the illustration relating to the individual Self. *yad etat gachchati iva cha manas*=the mind approaches or perceives, as it were, this Brahman. *anêna cha i.e.* and by means of the same mind. *êtat*=Brahman. *upasmarati* i. e. the devotee remembers, as if Brah-

1. The two analogies here given are intended to suggest, as pointed out in the commentary on the next passage, that Brahman—the Lord of the Universe—is almighty and can illumine the whole Universe in an instant. There is also a further suggestion that the act of creating the world is quite easy for Brahman—as easy as the opening or the closing of the eye is to us, because there is no obstacle whatever in the way of the Creator.

man were near. *abhīkshṇam*=incessantly. *saṃkalpaḥ* i.e. volition also points to Brahman. Because the mind conditions Brahman, decision, memory, and the like mental states indicate Brahman (as clearly) as if it is being perceived. Thus it forms an illustration referring to the individualised Self. The sense is that, as limited by divine adjuncts, (Brahman may be conceived as) showing itself suddenly like the light of lightning, the twinkle of the eye; and that, as limited by the individual's body, Brahman may be conceived as showing itself simultaneously with mental states. Thus illustrated, Brahman is comprehensible by the dull-witted and hence the statement of parallels. Surely, as unconditioned, it cannot be understood by the dull-witted[1].

Moreover,

6. That, verily, is what is known as 'the dearest of all' It is to be meditated upon as such (*tadvanam*). Whoever knows it thus—him, all beings seek.

Tat=Brahman. *ha*=verily. *tadvanam* i. e. is what all creatures cling to, as being their inner

---

1. The present illustration is given in order to point out how the Self—as residing in the human body—manifests itself through mental states of all sorts.

Self. Hence it is known as *tadvanam.* Because it is thus well-known it has to be meditated upon (*upâsitavyam*) as such—by referring to this particular feature. (The next part of the passage) states the results of such meditation. *saḥ yaḥ*=whoever. *ètat* i.e. Brahman of the said description. *èvam*=i. e. as possessing the said characteristic. *vêda* i.e. meditates upon. *ènam* i.e. such a devotee. *sarvâṇi*=all. *bhûtâni*=beings. *abhisamvânchhanti ha*=certainly seek, as indeed they do, Brahman itself.[1]

7. 'Please, sir, teach me the secret.' 'The secret has been taught to thee ; we have taught thee the secret relating to the supreme Brahman.'

Thus taught, the disciple asked the teacher as follows—*upanishadam* i. e. the secret that has to be pondered. *bhò*=sir. *brûhi*=say. *iti*=thus. When the disciple said so, the teacher replied—*uktâ*=has been taught. *tè*=to you. *upanishad*= (the secret). What is it then? The reply is—*Brâhmîm* i.e. relating to the supreme Self, for the instruction (given in sections i & ii) was in reference to the supreme Self. *vâva*=certainly. *upanishadam*

1. In accordance with the principle—*tadgunòpâsanèna tadèva phalam bhavati.*

abrûma iti—this merely reaffirms the substance of the answer (already given).

What is the intention of the pupil who (though) he has heard the secret (revealed) in respect of the supreme Self (still) asks—'Please, sir, tell me the secret?' If the question refers to what has already been imparted, it will be redundant and consequently, as useless as grinding what has already been well-ground. Or, if the secret, hitherto communicated, is incomplete, then it was not proper (for the teacher) to have concluded it by mentioning its final result (compare ii, 5.) (It has therefore to be understood that), as the matter has been closed once for all, the question cannot have reference to facts subsidiary to the teaching that has been imparted. What then can be the intention of the questioner ? It is this—Is there anything else needed—whether as a subordinate or as a co-ordinate aid[1], to secure the fruit of the knowledge that has been communicated ? Or, is it (what has been taught) whole in itself ? If it needs (any aid), then teach me the needed secret; if not, affirm, as Pippalâda (did)[2], that there is nothing more (required). According to this view we can well explain the teacher's affirma-

1. *ṣêshaṣabdêna phalôpakâryangamuktam*; *sahakâriṣabdêna anupasarjanamapi samuchchayârham vivakshitam.—Tîkâ.*

2. See *Praṣnôpanishad* vi, 7.

tion—that the secret has been revealed (to the disciple already).

Well, (what the teacher says here) cannot be termed an affirmation (at all) inasmuch as, in the next passage, he adds what remains to be added. True, the teacher (in the subsequent passage) says something that remains to be said, but what he says is not meant to be either a subordinate or a co-ordinate aid to the secret already communicated. It is only an external means for acquiring the knowledge of Brahman, as is patent from the fact that *tapas* &c. are associated, in that statement, with the *vêdas* and their *angas*. Neither the *vèdas* nor their *angas* like phonetics, for example, can be aids—subordinate or co-ordinate—in (securing the fruit of) Brahma-knowledge. If, however, it be urged that a proper apportionment of these should be made and that, as in the case of the *sûkta vâka mantras*[54] where a selection is made according to particular gods (invoked), *tapas* &c. should be taken as subordinate or co-ordinate aids (to Brahma-knowledge) and the *vêdas* and their *angas*

---

54. *Sûktavâka* is the name of a hymn, and in the *mantras* comprising it, are mentioned several deities such as *Agni*, *Agnishômau* and so on. These *mantras* are employed at the end of certain sacrifices but in employing them, variations are made in them according to the deity or deities invoked in the particular sacrifice.

—because they enable one to understand only the meaning (of *védic* texts),— as means of acquiring information. Such an apportionment is quite necessary because then only do we light upon a consistent meaning (of the passage). (We reply)— It cannot be so; for it is against reason. The apportionment indicated does not hold good, for Brahma-knowledge, which deems (as illusory) all notions of agency, fruit &c, cannot need any support— whether of a subordinate or of a co-ordinate kind. This knowledge is in reference to what is our inner Self which is abstracted from all empirical entities. So also is its fruit—final release[1]. Compare— 'Desiring liberation, one should give up all *karma* together with its aids. By such renunciation only can be known that which is the inmost essence of the person renouncing'. Hence knowledge cannot at all need *karma* as an aid and it is consequently wrong to resort to a separation of *satyam* &c. (from the *védas* &c.) as in the case of the *sûtravâka mantras*. The question and answer as re-affirming (what has already been stated) are quite appropriate (here) - Thus far has been stated the secret which does not depend upon anything else (for yielding its fruit of) immortality.

---

1. *Vidyâyâh vishayaparyâlôchanayâ phalaparyâlochanayâ cha nâsti tatvataḥ sambandhayôgyatâ (karmaṇâ)* —*Tîkâ*.

8. Its foundation is austerities, self-control, *karma*, the *Védas* and all their *angas*; truth (is its) abode.

Tasyai=*tasyâḥ*=of that secret relating to Brahman which we have taught you. *tapas* &c. are the means of acquiring knowledge[1]. *tapas* is control over body, mind and senses. *damaḥ*=calmness. *karma* i. e. *agnihôtra* and the like. Brahma-knowledge comes to one who is qualified by these and whose mind is pure. It is well-known that in the case of those whose sins are not at an end, Brahman, though explained, is not understood at all or only wrongly understood, as in the case of *Indra* and *Virôchana*. Therefore (it is said that) knowledge springs only in one whose mind has been purified by *tapas* and the like, practised in this or in many past births. Compare—' Whoever has full faith in the Supreme and whose faith in his teacher is as (great) as in the Supreme, to him only become clear these things when they are explained' (*Svèt*: *Up*: vi 23); ' Knowledge comes to those that are free from sin '. The word *iti* implies similar aids such as absence of pride, of

1. The *tîkâ* observes that the means mentioned are for the acquisition of the lower knowledge (as explained in the last two sections) as well as of the higher knowledge (as explained in the first two sections) or for knowing both the qualified and the unqualified Brahman.

vanity and so forth for acquiring Brahma-knowledge. *pratishthá*=feet i. e. as feet for this (knowledge). When they exist, Brahma-knowledge stands established as a man does on his feet. The four *vèdás* and all the six *angas*, such as phonetics, are also its foundation for it is the *vèdas* that enlighten us about *karma* as well as *jnána*, while the *angas* preserve (the *vèdas*). Or (we may say that) since the feet have been mentioned, the *védas* are all the remaining parts of the body (*sarvángáni*) as the head and so forth. In this interpretation, the *angas* should be understood as having been included under the term '*vedas*' itself. When the main thing is mentioned the subordinate ones, depending on it, are always understood. *satyam*=truth. *áyatanam* i. e. abode, where the *upanishad* rests. *satyam* is sincerity—absence of hypocrisy in thought, word and deed. Brahma-knowledge resides in people that are not hypocrites but are wholly virtuous and not at all in insincere people who are demon-like. Compare—' In whom there is no crookedness, no deception &c. (*Pra* : *Up* : i, 16). Hence *satyam* is stated to be the abode. Although *satyam* has been included under *tapas* and the rest, as feet, it is again mentioned as the abode for indicating its superiority as a means. Compare—'A thousand horse-sacrifices and Truth were weighed in the balance and Truth, though single, outweighed the thousand sacrifices'.

9. Whoever knows this, he, indeed, vanquishing sin, abides in the infinite, the highest heaven. He doth abide (there).

Yo vai=(whoever indeed). *ètâm* i. e., this Brahma-knowledge, taught in what begins with *kêna ishitam*. *evam*=i. e., thus highly valuable —as glorified in sections iii and iv and forming the basis of all knowledge whatsoever. *vèda*=(knows) though the result of Brahma-knowledge has already been mentioned it is repeated here for concluding the subject.[1] *apahatya*=having destroyed or shaken off. *pâpmânam* i. e., (sin or) the cause of mundane existence—ignorance, desire, and activity. *anantè*=endless. *svargê lokè* i. e., in Brahman which is of the nature of bliss. Since there is the qualifying word *anantè*, *svarga* does not refer to Heaven. Lest *anantê* be taken figuratively, it is added *jyéyé* i. e., great, superior to everything—i. e. the supreme Self. *pratitishṭhatê*=resides. The purport is that such an one does not come back to this changing world.

---

1. So that the last passage refers to the true knowledge of Brahman which forms the subject-matter of sections i and ii and which leads to complete liberation. The lower knowledge dealt with in sections iii and iv and which leads to *kramamukti* has been concluded already.

End of the Fourth Section.

MEMORIAL EDITION

of the works of

SRI SANKARACHARYA

20 Volumes
Crown 8vo.
in a teak case

Brahmasutrabhashya	**3 vols.**
Isa, Kena, Katha and Prasna Upanishad Bhashyas	**1 vol.**
Munda, Mandukya and Aitareya Upanishad Bhashyas	**1 vol.**
Taittiriya and Chhandogya Upanishad Bhashyas	**2 vols.**
Brihadaranyaka Upanishad Bhashya	**2 vols.**
Nrisimhatapani Upanishad Bhashya and Lalita Trisati Bhashya	**1 vol.**
Bhagavad-Gita Bhashya	**2 vols.**
Sahasranama and Sanatsujatiya Bhashyas	**1 vol.**
Vivekachudamani and Upadesasahasri	**1 vol.**

Minor Prakaranas	. **2 vols.**
Minor Stotras	. **2 vols.**
Prapanchasara and Miscellaneous .	. **2 vols.**

All the volumes are printed in the best style possible, illustrated with splendid half-tone and coloured pictures and are bound in cloth with a very attractive and elaborate design in gold. The twenty volumes are placed in a neat teak case and each case containing one complete set is priced at **Rupees FIFTY only** for those who register their names for the same before all the volumes are published. After that the price would be considerably raised since the cost of producing these volumes is enormous.

An **Edition de Luxe,** strictly limited to one hundred sets, is printed in very superior first quality Art paper and is bound in morocco with gilt edges and sides. This will be the most sumptuous edition of any Sanskrit book hitherto published, and is priced at **Rupees ONE HUNDRED only** per case of twenty volumes.

OPINIONS.

His Holiness, Sri Jagadguru Sri Sachchidananda Sivabhinava Nrisimha Bharati Swamigal, who adorns the throne of Sringeri, is graciously pleased to issue the following SRIMUKHA regarding this Memorial Edition.

अस्मदत्यन्तप्रियतमान्तेवासि कृष्णस्वामितनूभव बालसुब्रह्मण्यविषये श्रीनारायणस्मरणपूर्वकविरचिताशिषः समुल्लसन्तुतराम् ॥

श्रीमच्छुद्धाद्वैतविद्यासंप्रदायप्रवर्तकश्रीमच्छंकरभगवत्पादाचार्यदिव्यावतारपरिपूततमायां केरलान्तर्गतायां कालट्यां प्रवर्तिततदीयमूर्तिप्रतिष्ठामहोत्सवावसरे सहोत्साहं सश्रमं परिशोध्यासकृत् सहायेन पण्डितानां संमुद्य नागराक्षरैः स्फुटतरैरत्यन्तसुन्दरतमैश्च श्रीमदाचार्यभगवत्पादीयकृतीः सभक्तिश्रद्धं सप्रश्रयं भवत्समर्पिताः सहामोदमूरीकृत्य नितरामानन्दामहे ॥

जनयतश्च तृप्तिं रीतीमुद्रणपुस्तकयोः यथैव आचार्यभगवत्पादीयवाग्वैखरी ॥

आशास्महे वयमचिराद्यथा स्यात् समाप्तिः यावद्ग्रन्थमुद्रणस्य मुद्रितानां च ग्रन्थानां प्रचारः सर्वत्र जनेष्वास्तिकेष्वाचार्यभक्तिभरेषु तथा भवन्तमन्तेवासिनं भक्तवरम् अनुगृह्णन्तु श्रीमच्छारदाचन्द्रचूडादिदेवताः श्रीमदाचार्यभगवत्पादाश्चेति अलं पल्लवितेन ॥

The Madras Mail: —Sanskrit Scholars and Vedantic Students both in India and Europe, will be interested to hear that a complete edition of the works of Sri Sankaracharya, the great Hindu Reformer of South India, is announced by the SriVani Vilas Press, Srirangam. Mr. T. K. Balasubrahmanya Iyer, who has already done so much for the publication of old and rare Sanskrit Works, deserves to be congratulated on this idea of his. He has had the hearty co-operation of His Holiness, the present Sankaracharyar, of the Sringeri Mutt, Mysore, the modern representative of Sri Sankara himself at the seat he loved best, and numerous other Sanskrit Pundits and Scholars. The great Sankara is known to have written commentaries on all the twelve Upanishads, Brahma Sutras, the Bhagavad Gita, the Sahasranama and Sanatsujatiya. He is known to have devoted much attention also to the Prakaranas, and to have composed several popular hymns, besides many other works of a devotional and philosophic character. There has not hitherto been published a collected edition of all these works, and the present attempt of Mr. T. K. Balasubrahmanya Iyer is the first of its kind in India. Single works of the great Reformer have been printed at Mysore, Calcutta, and Bombay from time to time, but the greater portion of those mentioned are accessible to the student only in Mss. The present edition, besides giving as far as is now known, a complete collection of Sankara's works, will also possess the additional advantage of being a uniform series. We understand that several of the volumes are already printed, and that the rest are being rapidly pushed through the Press. The twenty volumes of 320 pages each, Cr. 8vo., will be distributed as follows:—Brahmasutra Bhashya, 3 vols.; the Upanishads, 7 vols.; Bhagavad Gita, 2 vols.; Sahasranama and Sanatsujatiya, 1 vol.; Vivekachudamani and Upadesasahasri 1 vol; Minor Prakaranas, 2 vols.; Minor Stotras, 2 vols.; Prapanchasara 1 vol.; Miscellaneous, 1 vol.

The Sri Vani Vilas Press is well known for its careful printing, and in keeping with its reputation, the above volumes will be printed in excellent style and bound in cloth with a very attractive and elaborate design in gold. The twenty volumes will be enshrined in a neatly made case, and each case containing one set will be priced **Rs. 50**.

An **Edition de Luxe** strictly limited to 100 sets is also to be printed on very superior art paper, and will be bound in Morocco with gold edges and sides. This will be the most sumptuous edition of any Sanskrit work hitherto published, and will be priced **Rs. 100**. per case of twenty volumes.

Hon. Mr. V. Krishnaswamy Aiyar, Member of the Council, Madras:— Mr, T, K. Balasubramania Iyer is bringing out a Memorial Edition of the works of Sri Sankaracharya. They will prove a fit offering at the shrine of the great Teacher at Kaladi, his birth-place, where a temple is being consecrated by his illustrious representative the Jagadguru of Sringeri. An Edition of the collected works of the saint, philosopher and poet will supply a want keenly felt by the lovers of Sanskrit and the students of the Advaita philosophy all over the world. Mr. T. K. Balasubramanya Iyer's reputation as a publisher is a guarantee for the success of this noble undertaking. He is fully entitled to the patronage of the discerning public. The specimen volumes give promise of a really handsome edition. I wish him complete success in his patriotic enterprize.

G. Gangadhara Somayajulu, *District Munsiff, Aska*:—The Memorial Edition of Sri Sankaracharya's works is unparallelled in the annals of indigenous book publication in India. The general get up of the books—the paper—the letter-press —the printing—the punctuation—the spaces between stanzas and paragraphs—the wieldy and tasteful size of the volumes—the artistic binding—the exhaustive tables of contents and indexes—and last though not least, the beautiful teak-wood book case within which the volumes are enshrined—have left nothing to be desired.

I have not seen another book in Sankrit published in India in the same style as these handy and charming volumes. Every lover of Sanskrit literature and every Public Library should, in my opinion, possess one set of these works. Great credit is due to the enterprising and energetic publisher Mr. T. K. Balasubrahmanya Aiyar B. A., who with commendable zeal and a great self-sacrifice appears to have made the publication of these volumes his life-task. Greater still should be the reverence due to His Holiness Sri Jagadguru Nrisimha Bharati Swamigal, the present head of the Sringeri Mutt for the initiative and encouragement given to the publisher for bringing out such an excellent edition of the Great Master's collected works.

M. S. Narayana Rao, Retired Deputy Commissioner, Bangalore—I received the parcel of Sri Sankaracharya's works. It is a pleasure to see them and to possess them.

Pulin Bihari Das, Asst. Accountant General, Bengal— The announcement of the publication was a real joy to me. The books that I have now by me are distinctly my pride and my admiration. I cannot adequately express how thankful I feel to you for putting me in possession of a treasure whose pure and serene rays have struck into the dark and made it ever phosphoroscent with an all-beautiful and all-beatific loveliness such as could not anywhere be found in Nature....................To me, I would again repeat, it is my joy and my pride, it is my only love and my only stay; in fine it is my soul itself.

Hon. T. V. Seshagiri Aiyar B. A., B. L., Madras—The volumes are very tastefully printed. They invite a man of even such poor attainments as myself to go through the works of the greatest intellect the world ever produced. I shall read the book and write to you again. The followers of Sri Sankaracharya owe a debt of gratitude to you which they can never sufficiently repay. I know you desire no praise. You have executed the work under the advise and inspiration of probably the worthiest of those that have been installed in the Peetam consecrated by the Founder of Advaitism.

M. R. Krishna Rao, retired Inspector-General of Registration, Trivandrum:—I have had the pleasure of receiving the parcel of the Memorial Edition of the works of Sri Sankaracharya. You have indeed rendered a great service to the Sanskrit-Reading members of the Advaita community by undertaking the publication of this collected edition. The execution is excellent in every way and leaves hardly anything more to be desired.

SRI VANI VILAS SASTRA SERIES.

---

1. **Adhvara Mimamsa Kutuhala Vritti** *of Sri Vasudava Dikshita*, Edited by S. KUPPUSWAMI SASTRIGAL M. A., Principal, Trivadi Sanskirt College, with the co-operation of Professors Brahmasri R. CHANDRASEKHARA SASTRIGAL and Brahmasri P. V. PANCHAPAGESA SASTRIGAL. Some of the note-worthy features of this edition will be found to be (1) the identification of quotations (2) a faithful representation of various readings and (3) a careful summary of each Adhikarana. When the work itself is completed, an exhaustive index and an elaborate introduction reviewing as perfectly as possible the Mimamsa Darsana itself in general and Kutuhala Vritti in particular will be given. To be completed in Thirty parts. Price of each part Cr. 4to. pp. vii—*56*. **Re 1.** Post

Free. [Prospectus and Specimen pages will be sent on application.]

Chapters I and II. Bound separately in cloth. Gilt lettered. Price **3 Rs. 8 As.** each. Post free.

[This Edition is specified as a Text Book for the M. A. Degree Examination of the Madras University.]

Hon. Dewan Bahadur Justice Sir Subramania Aiyar, B. L., L. L. D., K. C. I. E., Madras—My testimony to the value of the work to which you have so patriotically devoted yourself is hardly wanted considering the eulogistic notices which it has received from competent hands. I am sure your devotion to the cause of Sanskrit literature and to the dissemination of sound instruction through your Tamil Journal Sri Vani Vilasini will add credit to the University of which you are a graduate. I hope that your efforts will receive support from the Public.

Hon. P. S. Sivaswamy Aiyar, B.A., B.L., C. I. E , Advocate General and Chairman, Sanskrit Board of Studies, Madras. —Your edition of the Kutuhala Vritti is a scholarly work and the get-up is worthy of the reputation of your Press. You are fortunate in having secured the services of Mr. S. Kuppuswami Sastri M. A. the accomplished Principal of the Mylapore Sanskrit College and his two colleagues as editors of the work. I hope you will meet with encouragement in the publication of this treatise which is as lucid as it is comprehensive.

H. H. Kerala Verma, C.S.I., F. M. U., M. R.A.S., F. R.H.S., Valiya Koil Tampiran, Trivandram:—Like all the works issued from the Sri Vani Vilas Press, Kutuhala Vritti deserves all applause. It is beautifully got up and is sure to be hailed by all Pandits who take an interest in that profound Darsana 'Purva Mimamsa'.

T. Ganapati Sastri, Principal, Sanskrit College, Trivandrum:—Your undertaking is indeed a very gigantic and laudable one and I am glad to find that your work possesses all the requisites of an excellent edition............I shall also introduce it as a Text book in this College.

M. T. Narasimha Aiyangar, B.A., M.R.A.S., Bangalore.—You are rendering very valuable service to the literary public by undertaking the laborious task of bringing out this most important work on the Purva Mimamsa Sastra. The work is being edited with great care and the arrangement is very satisfactory.

The Hindu.—It gives us great pleasure to bring to the notice of the public the publication of this gigantic classic work, the first part of which has just reached us from the Sri Vani Vilas Press, Srirangam. The Indian Philosophy, classified as it is into the six systems or the *Shad Darsanas*, is the most important part of the literature of India and of Universal Philosophy. Of these six systems the *Purva Mimamsa of Jaimini* reduces to a system the Karma kanda of the Vedas. This *Kutuhala Vritti* is a commentary on the *Sutras of Jaimini* by the well-known scholar Vasudeva Dikshita presenting immense facilities for getting at the real significance of Jaimini's aphorisms. This work, besides representing in a lucid style the wealth of Sastraic informations given by the saintly Sabara Svamin, the vigorous Kumarila Bhatta, the learned Parthasarathi Misra and the scholastic Khanda Deva, gives a very close and careful interpretation of each of Jaimini's aphorisms with remarkable clearness and precision. That this extremely useful work is now brought to light for the first time, is due to the untiring efforts of the Sri Vani Vilas Press at the resuscitation of all that is rare and precious in the field of Sanskrit Literature. The work is edited by Mr. S. Kuppuswamy Sastrigal, M. A., Principal of the Madras Sanskrit College, with the co-operation of Professors Brahmasri R. Chandrasekhara Sastrigal and Brahmasri P. V. Panchapagesa Sastrigal, and consequently it is sure to be very carefully and accurately edited. It is based upon a collation of several manuscripts and the various differences in the readings are given in the foot-notes. An elaborate introduction reviewing as perfectly as possible the *Mimamsa Darsana* in general and *Kutuhala Vritti* in particular, is promised on the completion of the work. Printed on pure white antique paper, the letter-press and get-up is all that could be desired. Our readers may perhpas already know that the name of the Sri Vani Vilas Press is a guarantee for neatness and excellence in printing. As the work is priced cheap *viz.*, Re. 1 only, for each part, inclusive of all charges, we hope each and every Sanskrit scholar will go in for a copy and thus encourage the Press in its most laudable and patriotic undertaking.

2. Sariraka Mimamsa Sutra Bhashya by *Sri Sankara Bhagavatpadacharya* with BHAMATI by Vachaspati Misra, KALPATARU by Amalananda and PARIMALAM by Appayya Dikshita. [Details later on.]

3. Bhagavad Gita *With the Bhashya of Sri Ramanuja and the Tatparya Chandrika of Sri Vedanta Desika.* Edited by Rao Bahadur M. RANGACHARIAR M. A., Professor of Sanskrit, Presidency College, Madras, with the co-operation of A. V. Gopalachariar, M.A., B.L., and Pandit R. V. Krishnamachariar. To be completed in 16 parts. Cr. 4to. Price of the complete work, if paid in advance, **Rs. 6.** only. Postage One Rupee extra. Price of each part **As. 8.** per V. P. P. As. 10.

S. Kuppuswamy Sastrigal M.A., Principal, Sanskrit College Madras.—It goes without saying that this is the best edition of the Tatparya Chandrika which has yet appeared and after carefully going through the first part I have much pleasure in saying that this great work of Sri Vedanta Desika is being very carefully and accurately edited. The value of the Tatparya Chandrika bringing out in an excellent way the significance of Sri Ramanuja's words cannot be exaggerated. I have been feeling that Sri Vedanta Desika has done for Sri Ramanuja's works what Sri Appayya Dikshita and Sri Madhusudana Saraswati have done for Sri Sankara. All the Sanskrit Scholars are certainly much indebted to you for your patriotism and love of literature which prompt you every moment to bring out such excellent editions of such masterly works. I am sure that the blessing of the eminent sages and scholars, whom you are so sincerely worshipping by way of publishing and spreading their works in the best possible way, will never go in vain and every Indian who is proud of his invaluable heritage can never consistently forget what he ought to do for such good undertakings as yours.

M. T. Narasimha Aiyangar, B.A., M.R.A.S., Bangalore.—It is highly gratifying to see that the Sri Vani Vilas Press, Srirangam, has undertaken the publication of the Devanagari Edition of Bhagavad-Gita with Ramaunja-Bhashya and the Tatparya Chandrika of Vedanta Desikar. The 1st No. that was kindly sent to me by the Proprietor, shows that no pains have been spared to make the Edition attractive and eminently useful to the public. While the moderate price at which it is offered for sale, places it within the reach of the Pandit class also. The literary world knows how much scholars had to struggle to get at a correct reading of the hopelessly inaccurate Bangalore Edn. (in Telegu characters), for want of a better Edition. I believe the present Edition will be heartily welcomed by all Sanskrit scholars.

4. **Siddhanta Siddhanjanam** by Krishnananda Sarasvati with the commentary called Ratnatulika by Bhaskara Dikshita. To be edited by S. KUPPUSWAMY SASTRIGAL., M.A, Principal, Trivadi Sanskrit College. [Details later on.]

5. **Kavyalankarasutra Vritti** of Vamana with the commentary *Kamadhenu* of Gopendra Tippa Bhupala and with a critical Sanskrit Introduction. Royal 8vo. Pp. xviii-201 cloth gilt **Rs. 2-8.** Postage extra.

[This Edition is specified as a Text Book for the B. A. Degree Examination of the Madras University.]

The Hindu—The *Kavyalankara Sutra Vritti* is a well-known work on Sanskrit rhetoric by Vamana. The author represents a prominent school of thought in the subject, and the work is a scientific and artistic production, in the good old form of Sutras and Vritti. Vamana made the Sutras as well as the Vritti. This work of Vamana has already undergone more than one edition, but the present is undoubtedly a great improvement on all previous editions. The Sri Vani Vilas Press, Srirangam, have published this edition, and their name is a guarantee for everything excellent in publications of the kind. The publishers are no common literary critics and their Sanskrit introduction is a learned literary estimate of Vamana's work. Chapter by Chapter of the work is carefully reviewed, and several interesting questions connected with the work are raised and discussed. The important question of Vamana's date is considered at length. The publishers have shown great discrimination in the selection of the commentary known as "Kamadhenu" of Tippa Bhupala, the best commentary extant. The foot-notes are a noticeable feature of the book. The publishers are entitled to the gratitude of the Sanskrit loving public for their undertaking, and the University has already marked its recognition of the enterprise by prescribing this edition of the book as one of the text books for the B. A. Degree Examination.

6. **Brahmasutravritti** named *Brahma Tattva Prakasika* by the famous SADASIVENDRA SARASVATI with a sketch and a half-tone portrait of the author. Cr. 8vo. Pp. 322. cloth gilt **Rs. 2.** Postage extra.

The Wednesday Review—The book under review is a pre-eminently good guide for understanding the Brahmasutras. It is neither too short nor too long. The author has read deeply and digested all the literature on the subject and gives succinctly the broad features of each Adhikarana. * * Sadasiva-Brahma's commentary is a brilliant production. It will be of immense use alike to the unlearned student and to the deeply learned Pandit. The former can with its aid alone grasp clearly the meaning of the Sutras. The latter will find in the book the essence of all that is to be found in all the commentaries he has read. The author was not a mere book-worm, but a very great Yogi. He digested all his book-knowledge and lived the life of the Vedantin. He *realised* the truth of the teachings of the Vedanta. The work of such a great personage must necessarily be a model of clearness and sweetness. The spirit of the Yogi breathes through the whole work. * * The connection of the following Adhikarana with the foregoing one is explained fully throughout. At the end of a Pada or Adhyaya, the contents are briefly summed up in one or two slokas. The Vritti is one of the best works written in any language. The edition of the book by the Sri Vani Vilas Press is simply excellent. The editor has written an excellent life of the author. We commend the work to all readers of Sanskrit.

The Sri Krishna Review—We have much pleasure in acknowledging the receipt of a copy of this Sanskrit work, containing the original Vedanta-aphorisms by Vyasa, and a marvellously lucid commentary by Sadasivendra Sarasvati—one of the greatest of Rajayogins of Southern India. It is a volume of nearly 400 pages, printed in bold Sanskrit characters, and no pains have been spared to make it as attractive as possible The get-up of the book is simply excellent and the price of it **Rs.** 2 is remarkably cheap.

Kaviratna Jnanenda Chandra Chattopadhyaya, Lecturer in Sanskrit, Midnapore:—I sincerely thank you for the beautiful edition of a hitherto before unknown commentary, which I must say, is an invaluable acquisition to the store of Sanskrit learning.

7. **Sastra Darpana.** A masterly treatise on the Brahma Sutras by Amalananda, the author of Kalpataru. A *Unique* work in Sanskrit Literature. The author's splendid dessertation on each Adhikarana is a regular intellectual treat. Cr. 8vo. cloth gilt **Rs. 2-8.** Postage extra.

8. **Sutra Muktavali.** by Brahmananda, the author of Laghu Chandrika. [In the Press].

9. **Vedantasara of Sadananda** with the commentary of Apadeva and a critical English In-

troduction by Prof. K. SUNDARARAMA AIYAR AVL., M. A., Cr. 8vo. **Re, 1.** Postage extra.

The Theosophist:—To all lovers and followers of the Advaita, the famous Vedāntasāra of Sadānanda needs no introduction. Only half the book is devoted to this edition of Vedantasara and Apadeva's commentary; the other is a brilliant and convincing introduction by Prof. K. Sundararama Aiyar, M.A., of Kumbakonam. The Professor deals critically with Col. G.A. Jacob's and Doctor Thibaut's views on the Vedantasara. Both doubted that Shankara's doctrines could be supported by tradition, or even that Shankara evolved that tradition as authority, both doubted that the Upanishats and Badarayana could be claimed as authorities for Shankara's seeming independance of thought. Professor Sundararama shows that these two noted Scholars have mistaken the great Vedantic teacher, and refutes entirely their conclusions. If space permitted we would give a full discussion of the Professor's arguments. He clears these century-old yet ever interesting teachings from the misconceptions which has previously surrounded them.

10. **Purvottaramimamsa Vadanakshatramala** by the famous Appaya Dikshita. Cr. 8vo. **Rs. 2.** Postage extra.

11. **Yogasutravritti** named *Yogasudhakara* by the great Raja Yogin Sri Sadasivendra Sarasvati Cr. 8vo. **Re. 1. As. 8.** Postage extra.

12. **Bhagavad-Gita** with the commentary called 'Brahmanandagiri' of Venkatanatha. An excellent Advaitic commentary on the Gita. Cr. 8vo. Cloth Gilt. **Rs, 3-8.** Postage extra.

Sastra Booklets.

Siddhanta Kalpavalli. With the commentary called Kesara Valli by Sadasivendra Sarasvati. Cr. 8vo. **As. 8.** Postage extra.

Vyasatatparya Nirnaya by Ayyanna Dikshita Cr. 8vo. **As. 8.** Postage extra.

Lalita Trisati with the commentary of Sri Sankara Bhagavatpadacharya. Cr. 8vo. **As. 8** Postage extra.

Sarva Vedanta Siddhanta Sara Sangraha by Sri Sankara Bhagavatpadacharya. Cr. 8vo. **As. 8.** Postage extra.

Srutimatodyota by Tryambaka Sastri. Cr. 8 vo. **As. 6.** Postage extra.

Patanjala Darsana with the commentary of Ananta Pandita. Cr. 8vo. **As. 6.** Postage extra.

Uttara Gita. With the commentary of Sri Gauda-padacharya. Cr. 8vo. **As. 6.** Postage extra

Works Under Preparation.

Siva Gita with the commentary of Paramasivendra Sarasvati.

Upanishad Dipika by Sadasivendra Sarasvati.

Brahamamritavarshini by Ramananda.

Sesharya by Adisesha.

Taittiriyopanishad-Bhashya with the commentary named Vanamala.

Sri Vani Vilas Sanskrit Series.

1. **Parvati Parinaya** with a critical introduction and foot-notes by Pandit R. V. KRISHNAMACHARIAR. (With a Half-tone frontispiece of Parvati Parameswara.) Demy 8vo. pp. 18—71. Price **8 As.** Postage Extra.

Dr. E. Hultzsch Ph. D., Germany:—Please accept my best thanks for the copy of your new edition of the PARVATI PARINAYA which is excellent in every way. The text is much improved, the preface valuable and important and the get-up elegant. I am convinced that Pandit Krishnamachariar is right in attributing the drama to Vamana Bhatta Bana. Wishing your Series the success it fully deserves.

A. A. Macdonell Esq.. Boden Professor of Sanskrit, University of Oxford:—I have looked at your edition of the PARVATI PARINAYA and consider it to be the best edition of that play which has yet appeard. I hope the publications which will appear in the series which has been so well begun, will attain the same standard of excellence.

Justice Sarada Charan Mitra, Judge, High Court, Calcutta:—The Publisher deserves the sincerest thanks of all Indians. The paper and printing are also very good. This is a very laudable attempt of the SRI VANI VILAS PRESS.

Kali Krishna Goswami Vidyaratna M. A. Prof. of Sanskrit, D. A. V. College, Lahore:—Sanskrit publications of this kind are rarely to be seen, The paper, printing and make up of the book are excellent. It far surpasses the finish of Calcutta Bombay, Benares and Vizianagaram series publications. I offer my best thanks to Pandit Krishnamacharya who has so kindly compiled an able and excellent critical introduction and has appended a few necessary explanatory notes. The public, especially the scholar world would derive great benefit by such works if you continue to publish them in this way.

M. Rangachariar M.A., Professor of Sanskrit, Presidency College, Madras:—Your PARVATI PARINAYA is well printed and well edited. The introduction is very interesting......

K Ramanujachariar M.A., B.L., Principal, Maharaja's College, Vizianagaram:—The Introduction is very interesting The get-up is excellent. You will be placing under an obligation the Sanskrit-reading country by printing more books in this style.

R. Krishnamachariar M. A., Inspector of Sanskrit schools, Madras:—I congratulate you on the publication of your excellent edition of Parvati Parinaya. This is perhaps the first time that a Sanskrit Drama has been printed in such superior style in this Presidency. The able introduction to the work is very instructive and indicates the extent of the analytical faculty of the Pandit.

The Madras Mail:—PARVATI PARINAYA is the title of a well-known Sanskrit drama with an introduction and brief notes by Pandit R. V. Krishnama Chariyar. In the Sanskrit introduction, the popular belief that this drama was composed by Bhatta Bana, the celebrated author of *Kadambari* and *Harsha Charita*, is sought to be refuted and the theory advanced that Vamana Bhatta Bana, who is said to have lived in the fifteenth century, was the real author. The printing and get up of the book reflect credit on the *Sri Vani Vilas Press* at Srirangam, which is responsible for its publication.

V. Krishnaswamy Aiyar B. A., B. L., Judge, High Court Madras:—I congratulate you on the exceedingly well printed edition of 'PARVATI PARINAYA' brought out by you. I have rarely seen Sanskrit books printed so well in southern India.

Dr. R. Schmidt in the Indian Antiquary:—The new collection of Sanskrit texts, of which this work is the first instalment, has just been started by Mr. T. K. Balasubramanyam B. A., of Srirangam. Although the drama *Parvati Parinaya* has no poetical value at all, but is nothing but a tiresome and unsavoury rechauffe of an old story that had been charmingly told by Kalidasa in his *Kumarasambhava*, the new edition forms a very interesting contribution to literary history inasmuch as the editor, Pandit R. V. Krishnamachariar in his elaborate and flowing *Bhumika* or introduction, discusses at length the authorship of the *Parvati Parinaya* and the date of its author. On the strength of æsthetical and historical arguments, Mr. Krishnamachariar, disproves the popular

belief that the author of *Kadambari* and *Harsha Charita* composed the *Parvati Parinaya* as well, and attributes this drama to a certain Vamanabhattabana, who lived in fifteenth century A.D., Bana being only the abridged form of Vamanabhattabana. That the *Parvati Parinaya* belongs to a pretty late time, is first concluded by Mr. Krishnamachariar from the *argumentum ex silentio:* no writer on Sanskrit rhetorics or poetics ever cites the *Parvati Parinaya.* Of course, we could not rely on such an argument alone but there are others, taken from inscriptions and literature, which show that Vamanabhattabana, the author of the *Viranarayanacharita*, the *Sabdaratnakara*, the *Sringarabhushanabhana*, &c., sprung from the Vatsa family, and bearing the *biruda* Abhinavabana, is the author of the *Parvati Parinaya* too. This poet was the *protégé* of the Reddi king Vema *alias* Viranarayana, whose time is fixed by some inscriptions; see *Bhumika.* p. 10 ff.............. As regards the text of the present edition, I have found it to contain several good *variæ lectiones*, by comparing it with the pervious texts......................
The publisher is quite right when he says that "The publication of this Sanskrit Series needs no justification," and "Readers of this edition of Parvati Parinaya will observe the various differences in the readings and also note what vast improvements have been effected thereby." Our thanks are, I consider, due to him and to the learned editor.

Vasavadatta *of Subandhu*— with a full a exhaustive commentary by Pandit R. V. KRISHNAMACHARIAR. The text is very carefully edited in consultation with several ancient Mss. and the commentary is quite exhaustive and is written in very simple and elegant style. The following slokas from the commentary will give an idea of its nature.

The book is printed in the best style possible in Cr. 8vo. size on good antique paper and the get-up leaves nothing to be desired. Pp. v, lxvi—359. Price **Rs. 2.** Postage Extra.

N. B.—This book is specified by the Madras University as the edition to be followed for the B. A. Degree Examination.

The Hindu :—This is the first Sanskrit Prose work extant and it is strange that there was no good edition at all of this work up to now. The two Grantha editions and the only Telugu edition that are now available in the market are not worth the name of an edition at all. They contain an apology of a commentary and are printed in the worst style possible. The only Devanagari edition with Sivarama's commentary is equally unsatisfactory both in the text and the commentary. As a matter of fact, portions of the text are altogether omitted in this edition. On the other hand, the book before us which forms the second of the Sri Vani Vilas Sanskrit Series, is considerably improved. As stated in the preface, there is no doubt that considerable care has been bestowed in choosing the happiest readings possible on all occasions. Secondly the commentary is quite full and exhaustive, particular attention having been paid to test the author's statement that he has used *slesha* throughout the work. In short, the commentary is very scholary and interesting and reflects great credit on the commentator. Last but not least, the get-up is very fine and most attractive. Printed beautifully in Crown 8vo. size on white Antique paper the book is very attractive.

Louis H. Gray, Newark, U.S.A.—I can very conscientiously say that it is one of the most admirable editions I have ever seen from an Indian press and the commentary of Pandit Krishnamachariar, has my unstinted praise.

Justice S. C. Mitra, Calcutta.—I am glad to say that the edition is very good. I have gone through the whole of the part sent to me and I find the notes useful.

M. Rangachariar, M. A., Professor of Sankrit, Presidency College, Madras :—I see that already the Sri Vani Vilas Press has acquired a wide and well deserved fame for the excellently artistic and accurate work that it has turned out. Your edition of VASAVADATTA should prove very useful to students as well as to Teachers. I have heard portions of the commentary read to me. It is learned, ingenious and generally interesting. The endeavour to intrepret the language of Subandhu in accordance with the expression of his own *Pratigna* is well worth making even though our success may happen to be less than full.

S. Kuppuswamy Sastriar, M. A., Principal, Sanskrit College, Madras :—I find that this book is very carefully edited and no pains have been spared to pick out and adopt the best readings. The intelligent commentary of Pandit R. V. Krishnamacharya gives a lucid and beautiful paraphrase of many passages and clears many difficulties which are left unsolved by the other commentaries. I think that this is the only commentary where an earnest attempt is made to bring out what Subandhu might have really meant and to minimise the necessity for resorting to forced interpretations. I would gladly recommend this edition to all the students of Vasavadatta and I am sure they will be much benefitted by following this edition and this commentary.

Rev. M. Phillips, Madras.—The book is well got up and the commentary reflects great credit on the care and scholarship bestowed upon it.

Honorable P. S. Sivaswamy Aiyar, B. A., B. L., Madras.—It goes without saying that your publications are excellently well got up quite unlike the course unattractive style of Sanskrit Publications generally. You are doing a very useful service to the country by bringing out handsome editions of Sanskrit Classics and rare works.

H. H. Kerala Varma C. S. I., F.M.U., M.R.A.S., F. R. H. S., Valiya Kovil Tampiran, Trivandram.—You deserve great credit for bringing out Vasavadatta so very nicely.

3. **Priyadarsika** with commentary and Bhumika by Pandit R. V. KRISHNAMACHARIAR. (With a Half-tone frontispiece of Priyadarsika.) Demy 8vo. pp. XLVIII—97. Price **12. As.** Postage Extra.

The introduction in Sanskrit is written purposely in easy flowing style, easily understandable by all the students and discusses very ably the authorship, the date and other such very important details. This is more exhaustive than the one for Parvati Parinaya which has been spoken of very highly by all the scholars both from the West and the East. A short *resumé* of this Introduction is given in English also.

R. C. Dutt, C. I. E.—The discussion as to the authorship of Priyadarsika is very interesting and valuable.

S. Kuppuswamy Sastriar, M. A., Principal, Sanskrit College, Madras :—Your love of literature in having brought out such excellent editions of these Sanskrit Dramas (Parvati Parinaya and Priyadarsika) deserves all kinds of recognition at the hands of all lovers of Sanskrit literature. I find much care has been bestowed upon the typographical execution of these works and they speak volumes in favour of the Sri Vani Vilas Press. I have carefully gone through the learned Introductions to these Dramas and I am fully convinced of the unique attainments of Pandit R. V. Krishnamachariar. The intelligent way in which the learned Pandit combines the time honoured Sastraic ideals of Sanskrit literary criticism with the ideals of the modern Scientific criticism cannot fail to command the respect of all substantial Sanskrit scholars and to make them think that in these days when original capacity for intelligent and methodical criticism rarely manifests itself especially among pandits, Pandit R. V. Krishnamachariar may be very reasonably considered to figure as an isolated instance with sufficient capacity to prove to the literary world what an intelligent Sanskrit scholar with a keen critical acumen may do for the resuscitation or for a correct appreciation of Sanskrit Literature.

4. **Yadavabhyudaya** of *Sriman Vedanta Desika* with the commentary of the renowned *Appayya Dikshita.* (Illustrated with several Half-tones.) This work which consists of 24 Cantos will be published in 6 Vols. of 4 Cantos each.

Vol. I Cantos 1—4 With the life of Sri Vedanta Desika by A. V. GOPALACHARIAR, M.A., B.L., Cr. 8vo. xxxiv—240. **1 Re. 8 As.** Postage Extra.

Vol. II Cantos 5—8 With the life of Sri Appayya Dikshita. Cr. 8vo. Pp. xxxii—259. **1 Re. 8 As.** Postage Extra.

Vol. III Cantos 9—12. [In the Press.]

Justice S. C. Mitra, Calcutta.—The paper and printing are very good and the life of Vedanta Desika contains valuable informations. It suggests to me the writing of a history of Vijayanagaram. My thanks are also due to Mr. Gopalachariar M.A., B.L., The books published by the Sri Vani Vilas Sanskrit Series Editors are almost new to Bengal and they throw a flood of light on the history of literature of the Middle Ages in Southern India. The age was dark in Northern India, but it was not so in the south, apparently owing to the existance of the Hindu Kingdom of Vijayanagaram.

Rao Bahadur, M. Rangachariar, M.A., Professor of Sanskrit, Presidency College, Madras.—Many thanks for your excellent edition of the Yadavabhyudaya.

S. Krishnaswamy Aiyangar, M A., M.R.A.S., Bangalore.—Kindly allow me to thank you for the nice little volume of your excellent edition of the first four Sargas of Sriman Vedanta Desika's Yadavabhyudayam with the commentary of the revered Appiah Dikshita. You are doing invaluable service to Sanskrit Literature by bringing out the works of this great author, which till now, having been obtainable in wretched books in Telugu or Grantha Characters only had so far been unknown practically to scholars outside of South India. This highly gratifying duty you have done in a way which deserves all commendation and I hope you will have a sufficiently encouraging reception to enable you to continue the good work thus begun and bring out a complete set of the great author's work.

N. V. Desikachariar, M.A., B.L.,—I have read with great pleasure your edition of Yadavabhyudaya. The Idea of publishing such rare works in Sanskrit is very praiseworthy. There are many smaller treasures in Sanskrit which unhappily are hidden. You are rendering great public service by publishing them in the attractive form that you have done. Nothing is more calculated to popularise them than decent presentation. The appearance of a series of pictures of Sri Krishna that Immortal Child, to whom our hearts are so closely wedded, enhances the utility of the book. I should congratulate you on your arranging to publish English essays similar to the one that appears in the present volume. I am quite sure this edition will prove very popular amongst lovers of Sanskrit not only in India but in western countries also. The get up of the book is well suited to the merits of the work. The reputation of Sri Vedanta Desika, the lion of poets and disputants is somewhat local. Your edition will surely extend his well-merited fame. I am eagerly looking forward to the pleasure of going through the other volumes you intend publishing.

M. T. Narasimha Aiyengar, B.A., M. R. A. S., Bangalore.—I heartily congratulate you on the unparallelled success which has attended your noble efforts in bringing out a Devanagari edition of this great work. The neat execution of the printing, with apt illustrations, and the scholarly English Introduction leave little to be desired to make the publication attractive and useful. I am sure the Sanskrit reading public will thankfully acknowledge your services towards the advancement of Sanskrit Literature, by extending their ready patronage to your publications. I hope the neat publication of this volume will mark an era in the editing of Sanskrit works in India.

R. C. Dutt, C.I.E,—The Yadavabhyudaya has been excellently got up and the illustrations are good. I hope it will soon be completed.

The Hindu.—The Sri Vani Vilas Press. Srirangam, has again laid the Sanskrit-knowing world under a deep dept of gratitude by issuing an excellent edition in *Devanagari* of this splendid poem with the famous commentary of the renowned Appaya Dikshit.

The poem is a *Mahakavya* in 24 cantos by Sri Vedanta Desika the reputed Sri Vaishnava Acharya who lived in Southern India during 13th and 14th centuries. The poem has thus the unique distinction of being composed by a great popular Visishtadvaita Acharya and being commented upon by an equally distinguished leader of a rival school of Philosophy whose lifework was to refute the tenets of the School to which the author of the poem belonged. Both the text and the commentary are now published for the first time in Devanagari, a character known throughout the world; and hence, the well merited fame of Vedanta Desika, which, till now, was more or less confined to southern India, will spread far and wide to the immense delight of all Sanskrit Scholars. His compositions richly deserve to be more widely known and appreciated. The present edition is carefully edited from a collation of several Mss. and the system of punctuation adopted in the commentary is such as to make it easily understandable by all. Mr. T. K. Balasubramania Aiyer is certainly doing invaluable service to Sanskrit Literature by bringing out such rare and excellent works. Regarding the printing and get-up, we can only say that it is always a pleasure to handle books issued from the Sri Vani Vilas Press, Srirangam. The first volume containin the first four cantos is now published, and we are sure the other volumes also will be eagerly expected one after the other. It was a happy idea to have given an introduction to each volume in English and the life of Desika by Mr. A. V. Gopalachariar, M.A., that appears in this first volume is very well and exhaustively written. It is stated that the subsequent volumes will contain the life of Appaya Dikshita, origin and growth of Kavya Literature, Sri Desika as a poet, and a critical estimate of Yadavabhyudaya, etc. We wish all success to this undertaking and hope every Sanskrit-knowing gentleman will patronise the publication in all possible ways.

Hon. P. S. Sivaswamy Aiyar, B.A., B.L., Madras—It was a pleasure to me to look into the pages of your edition of the Yadavabhyudayam. It is splendidly got up and compares favourably with the best Sanskrit Publications in European countries. Mr. A. V. Gopalachariar's preface gives a very interesting account of the author's life and works.

The Theosophist, Madras—Yadavabhyudaya published by the Sri Vani Vilas Pres, Srirangam, contains a clear and correct account in English of Vedantacharya's life, a critical estimate of his literary and other works and also the learned commentary of Appaya Dikshita, the well known author of Rhetoric, written in the middle of the sixteenth century. It is clearly printed, pleasant to the eyes and its form and price make it convenient to possess.

Sanskrit study is rapidy growing in interest partly owing to the quickening stimulus of the Indian Universities, and partly also to the cheap and well printed publication of Sanskrit classics. We have no doubt that rare Sanskrit works—with multiplicity of readings so difficult to edit without the skilled experience of trained Pandits—coming out of this Press, in rapid succession, mark an increasing demand of neat edition which the modern resources of good type, good paper and illustrations make possible, and is also an excellent sign of a general progress in Sanskrit culture. The editor of this rare work is to be congratulated on the thoroughly accurate and scholarly publication which has the peculiar interest of being the literary attempt of a renowned theologian. In the selection and the treatment of the subject, both in this work and in the more popular Hamsasandesa, the imitation of Kali dasa is so apparent that almost any verse taken at random can be easily found to have its parallel in Raghuvamsa and Meghasandesa. We may instance the address of Devas and Earth to Vishnu in the ocean of milk and description of Devaki's pregnancy. The charm of freshness of thought and clear cut phrases give place to inevitable artificiality of conception and form and a rigid adherence to the orthodox rules of Sanskrit rhetoric. The commentary is full and learned and at the same time clear and practical and no doubt will be appreciated by advanced Students of Sanskrit literature.

5. **Malavikagnimitra.** With the commentaries of *Nilakantha* and *Katayavema*, and an English Introduction. Demy 8vo. XXVIII—155. Price **As. 12** only. Postage Extra.

6. **Achyutarayabhyudaya** *of Sri Rajanatha* with a commentary by Pandit R. V. Krishnamachariar. To be completed in 2 parts. This is a rare historical Kavya not published hitherto. Part I. Cantos 1—6. Cr. 8vo. pp. iv—156. **Re. 1** Postage Extra. (This book is prescribed as one of the text books for the F. A. Examination of the Madras University).

Part II. Cantos 7—12. [In the Press].

The Hindu:—We must apologise to the Sri Vani Vilas Press for not having been able to review promptly this rare historical Kavya of a famous poet Sri Rajanatha by name who is said to have lived in the 16th century. This work treats of the exploits of Achyutaraya, one of the emperors of the "Never-to-be-forgotten" Empire—Vijayanagar. It is only the first part that is now before us, but the second is promised very shortly with a critical introduction from the able pen of Prof. M. Rangachariar, which is bound to be excellent. The publishers have taken care to put in the best readings after consulting some 5 or 6 different Manuscripts. The commentary is very simple and lucid. In this connection we must put in a word of praise about Mr. T. K. Balasubrahmanyam for his untiring efforts to bring to light old Sanskrit works which, though highly valuable, are nothing in the sacred corner of a pandit's habitation or in the innermost recesses of an oriental palace. The get up of the book is excellent, and we hope lovers of Sanskrit will fully appreciate the value of the work.

A. A. Macdonell Esq., Boden Professor of Sanskrit, University of Oxford.—I have just received copies of numbers 3 and 6 of the Sri Vani Vilas Sanskrit series, the Priyadarsika and the Achyutarayabhyudaya with commentaries by Pandit R. V. Krishnamachariar. The books seem to be well and carefully printed maintaining the standared set up by the first number.

S. Kuppuswamy Sastriar, M. A., Principal, Sanskrit College, Madras,—I find that Rajanatha is one of those few poets who appear in the last days of the Kavya Literature and who do not sacrifice the Reeti and Rasa to merely ornamental verbiage. The style is good and the work teems with striking poetic images. Being a historical Kavya somewhat more difficult than Raghuvamsa and less difficult than Magha, I think it may serve as a suitable text book for the F.A. Standard. The commentary is clear and precise.

7. **Kamalinikalahamsa** by Raja Chudamani Dikshita (in the Press).

8. **Sankara Vijayam** by Sri Vidyaranya with the commentary called Dindima by Dhanapati Suri. Cr. 8vo. (in the Press).

9. **Uttararamacharita** of Bhavabhuti with the commentary of Narayana Bhattapada. (in the Press).

10. **Subhashita Nivi** of Sri Vedanta Desika, with the commentary called Ratnapetika. Edited by M. T. Narasimha Aiyangar, B.A., M.R.A.S., Central College, Bangalore. Cr. 8vo XII—106, 4. **As. 8.** Postage extra.

Justice Sarada Charan Mitra, Calcutta.—It is a work of considerable merit and the readers of Sanskrit Philosophy should all thank you for its publication. The preface and the Introduction deserve study. Every gentleman with a knowledge of Sanskrit should have a copy of it.

The Madras Mail.—This is a well-known Sanskrit didactic master-piece of Vedantadesika, the great Vaishnava teacher who appears to have lived during the 13th and 14th centuries A.D. The poem is a short one, but is printed with its commentary, Ratnapetika by Srinivasa Suri, who wrote about 1385 A.D. Vedanta Desika is known to have composed it for the special edification of prince Singappa Naick one of the earlier Venkatagiri Chiefs. It inculcates moral and philosophical ideas by the artful use of allegory. The style is dignified and the ideas are lofty. Mr. M. T. Narsasimha Iyengar, B.A., M.R.A.S., of the Central College, Bangalore, writes an interesting historical Introduction to the work. He must be congratulated on the excellent edition he has brought out.

11. **Ratnavali** *of Sri Harsha*. (In the Press).

12. **Guruvamsakavya** of *Lakshmana Sastri* with his own commentary called Bhavabodhini. A very rare work treating of the line of Jagadgurus in the Sringeri mutt beginning from Sri Sankara Bhagavatpada. Edited by Brahmasri KRISHNA SASTRIGAL, Dharmadhikari of Mysore and of Sri Sringeri Mutt. (In the Press).

13. **Sakuntala** of Kalidasa with the commentary of ABHIRAMA. With several Half-tone Illustrations (In the Press.)

14. **Raghuvamsa** of Kalidasa with the commentary of Arunagirinatha to be published in 3 vols. Cr. 8vo. Vol. I. Cantos 1—6. (In the Press).

15. **Meghasandesa** of Kalidasa with the elaborate and critical commentary 'Vidyullata' by

Purna Sarasvati. Cr. 8vo. Pp. xii—188 Cloth bound. Gilt. **Re. 1.** Postage extra.

16. **Vemabhupalacharitam** otherwise known as Veeranarayanacharitam. A Historical prose work by Vamana Bhatta Bana with an Introduction in Sanskrit by R. Krishnamachariar, M.A. Cr. 8vo. Pp. xv—235. Cloth bound: Gilt. **Rs. 2.** Postage extra.

17. **Chandraloka** with the commentary of Saradagama (in the Press).

18. **Sivalilarnava** of Sri Nilakantha Dikshita with Eight half-tone and coloured illustrations and with an Introduction on 'Nilakantha Dikshita and his contemporaries' by T. S. KUPPUSWAMY SASTRIGAL of Tanjore. Cr. 8vo. Pp. 48—487. Cloth bound: Gilt. **Rs. 2-4.** Postage extra.

19. **Nilakantha Vijaya Champu** by Sri Nilakantha Dikshita (In the Press.)

20. **Gangavatarana** A kavya by Sri Nilakantha Dikshita. (In the Press.)

Works Under Preparation.

Sankarabhyudaya Kavya by Rajachudamani Dikshita.

Jivanmuktikalyana Natakam by Nalla Dikshita.

Sankaramandara Saurabha Champu by Nilakantha.

Anandaraghavam A Drama by Rajachudamani Dikshita.

Jagadguru Champu by Kavi Varadachar.

Nalacharitram A Drama by Nilakantha Dikshita.

Minor Works of Nilakantha Dikshita.

Natesa Vijayam

SAHASRANAMA SERIES.

Stotras and Archana alone: Very useful for Parayanam. Demy 16mo. Price 4 As. each. Postage Extra.

1. Lalita Sahasranama.
2. Vishnu Sahasranama.
3. Lakshmi Sahasranama.
4. Vedasara Sivasahasranama.
5. Hanumat Sahasranama.
6. Subrahmanya Sahasranama.

TWO ANNAS LIBRARY OF SANSKRIT STOTRAS.

1. Soundarya Lahari by Sri Sankara Bhagavatpadacharya.
2. Sivananda Lahari by Do.
3. Akhyashashti and Sivabhaktikalpalatika by Sri Sridhara Venkatesarya, otherwise known as Tiruvasanallur Aiyyaval.
4. Sadasivendrastuti by the present Sri Jagadguru of Sringeri, with a portrait of Sadasiva Brahma.
5. Sarada Stotras by Do.
6. Sarada Navaratri Stotras by Do.
7. Miscellaneous Stotras Part I by Do.
8. Do. Part II by Do.
9. Do. Part III by Do.
10. Dayasatakam by Sri Sridhara Venkatesarya.
11. Do. by Sri Vedanta Desika.
12. Bhujanga Stotras by Sri Sankara Bhagavatpada.
13. Mahimna Stotras—Sakti Mahimna by Durvasas and Siva Mahimna by Pushpadanta.

14. Stotras of Sri Vedanta Desika Part I.
15. Do. Part II.
16. Lalitastavaratnam by Durvasas.
17. Aryasatakam by Muka Kavi.
18. Padaravindasatakam Do.
19. Stutisatakam Do.
20. Katakshasatakam Do.
21. Mandasmitasatakam. Do.
22. Guruparamparastotras.
23. Matribhutasataka by Sri Sridhara Venkatesarya.

'PRECIOUS GEM BOOKLETS'

A Series of dainty little books containing precious gems from Sanskrit Literature. In several cases these booklets are adorned with gems of Art. Very handy. Each **As. 3/** only. Postage extra.

1. **Poems of Kalidasa.**
    1. **Meghasandesa.**
    2. **Ritusamhara.**
    3. **Kumarasambhava cantos 1 and 2.**
    4. Do. Do. **3 and 4.**
    5. Do. Do. **5 and 6.**
    6. Do. Do. **7.**
    7. **Raghuvamsa cantos 1 and 2.**
    8. Do. Do. **3 and 4.**
    9. Do. Do. **5 and 6.**
    10. Do. Do. **7 and 8.**
    11. Do. Do. **9 and 10.**
    12. Do. Do. **11 and 12.**
    13. Do. Do. **13 and 14.**
    14. Do. Do. **15 and 16.**
    15. Do. Do. **17, 18 & 19.**
2. **Songs of Sri Sadasiva Brahmendra.**

OTHER SANSKRIT BOOKS.

	Rs. A. P.
Sarasvati Stotra, Syamala Dandaka and Navaratnamala *by Kalidasa*, Artistically printed in two colours. Royal 32mo. 2nd Edition. Handy pocket size.	0 1 0
Price per 100 copies. ...	5 0 0
Siva Dandaka by Bhaskararaya and **Sivashtaka**	0 1 0
Atmavidyavilasa of Sri Sadasiva Brahmendra. ...	0 2 0
Govindashtaka of Sri Sankara Bhagavatpada with 8 halftone illustrations ...	0 2 0
Achyuta Sataka: A Prakrit poem by Sri Vedanta Desika with the chchaya. ...	0 2 0
Raghuvamsa Cantos 10 and 11. Text only. ...	0 3 0
Bhagavad Gita. Text alone in bold characters. Printed on fine white antique paper. Very useful for parayanam. 100 pages Royal 8vo.	0 4 0

The Hindu :—We have received from the Sri Vani Vilas Press, Srirangam, a fine edition of Bhagavad Gita printed in bold Devanagari types on pure white paper. Each half of a sloka is given in a separate line and the get up is all that could be desired. The whole book covers 104 pages and the price, *viz.* 4 as. only per copy is very cheap.

Hon. P. S. Sivaswamy Aiyar, B.A., B.L., Madras—Your edition of the Bhagavad Gita is splendid and worthy of our national treasure.

Bhagavad-Gita. Text alone. Pocket Edition. 0 4 0

Vivekachudamani by Sri Sankara Bhagavatpadacharya. Text alone. Pocket Edition. F. Cap. 8vo. 118 pages. ... 0 4 0

Champu Ramayanam—*Kishkindhakandam.* With a lucid commentary. Cr. 8vo. ... 0 4 0

Satakas of Bhartrihari containing the Niti, Vairagya and Sringara Satakas. ... 0 6 0

Vishnupadadikesantastotram With the commentary of Purna Sarasvati ... 0 8 0

Panchasati by Muka Kavi 0 8 0

Sahridayananda: by Krishnananda, Cantos 1—6 with a commentary by Pandit M. C. SATAGOPACHARIAR, Royal 12mo. 0 12 0

Works of Sri Sacchidanada Sivabhinava Nrisimha Bharati Swami, the present Jagadguru of Sringeri. Part I. with three half-tone portraits. ... 1 0 0

Sahitya Ratna Manjusha: A collection of familiar quotations from the various Sanskrit Dramas, Kavyas and Prose literature by Pandit R. V. KRISHNAMACHARIAR. This book consists of 4 parts, the 1st containing the prose quotations from the Dramas, the 2nd, the poetical quotations, the 3rd, quotations from the Prose Literature and the 4th from the Kavyas. Cr. 8vo. pp. 181. 1 0 0

The Hindu :—This is a collection of wise sayings culled from the several masterpieces of Sanskrit authors. It is, like the well-known Bartlett's Familiar Quotations, a very useful book of reference containing as it does all the general maxims that are found scattered among the several works of Sanskrit literature. This is the first attempt of its kind in Sanskrit and the Sri Vani Vilas Press, Srirangam which has issued this extremely useful book should certainly be congratulated on its labours in the field of Sanskrit literature. Students especially will find this publication very helpful in their composition and translation work. We should also recommend it to every school and College library where we are sure it will be much used by the students. The price *viz.*, Re. 1 per copy is moderate enough considering the labour involved.